THE
SEARCH

BY CHRIS STEFANICK
AND PAUL McCUSKER

AUGUSTINE INSTITUTE

Augustine Institute
6160 S. Syracuse Way, Suite 310
Greenwood Village, CO 80111
Tel: (866) 767-3155
augustineinstitute.org

Cover Design and Layout: Ben Dybas

Printed in Canada

CONTENTS

ACKNOWLEDGMENTS

The authors would like to express their gratitude to those whose ongoing prayers and generosity made this project possible:

- John and Margaret Kelly
  Kelly Family Charitable Fund

- Anonymous

- Mark and Nancy Bauman

- Brian and Erin Kelly
  Kelly Family Foundation

We're also deeply appreciative to the many experts who gave us the benefit of their knowledge and wisdom in the pages of this book and on-camera for the video series.

We live in a time of unprecedented technological progress. In a relatively short time, we've seen our social, moral, and technological assumptions break away from their foundations. The engineers of this new reality offer us remarkable opportunities for personal happiness, fulfillment, and connectedness. Or so it would seem.

Yet, for all of the changes we've seen, people don't seem happier, more fulfilled, or better connected. We are still asking the same questions that have been asked by every generation since humans arrived on the scene. Who am I? Why do I exist? What is the point of my life?

Socrates observed that the unexamined life is not worth living. He provoked those who simply wanted to go with the flow, who reduced living to being comfortable. Socrates was steadfast in his pursuits. He knew there was more to life than his contemporaries seemed to believe. He was always questioning. He was constantly searching.

Life is more than comfort. Life is more than a checklist of accomplishments and activities. While such a list might help you fill out a college or job application, it does not fill up your heart. Every life is a story, and a life without a purpose is like a story without a plot. Each of us needs, especially in moments of pain and hardship, to discover the purpose of our life.

As children we often asked "*why?*" Why do we seem to stop asking? This is the wisdom of Socrates; he knew that every life is a story in search of a plot. He was the radical one who never stopped asking *why*. And you can't find the *why* without tackling those often provocative and uncomfortable questions. But once you abandon comfort-seeking and take up the larger and more interesting quest for purpose, a new horizon opens up before you.

Because of these questions, the Augustine Institute has created *The Search*. With the dynamic and insightful Chris Stefanick as our guide, *The Search* explores the answers to the core questions of life, with clarity, credibility, and a healthy dose of humor along the way.

Whether you're wildly optimistic or a jaded skeptic, *The Search* will speak to you. You may be reassured by some parts, and challenged by others. Either way, you'll find a lot to think about. And when all is said and done, life's questions will demand to be answered.

Are you ready for *The Search*?

Tim Gray
President, The Augustine Institute

CHAPTER ONE

WHAT ARE YOU LOOKING FOR?

We're on a journey—the ultimate journey: *life.*

We experience both the mountaintops and the valleys; we take in the air all around us. But whether you're up at the top or down at the bottom, we are all on the same journey.

Have you ever stopped to ask yourself—as you speed through the years—where we're all going? What is this journey that begins the moment we were conceived? Does the road ahead consist of randomly wandering through time, or is there a destination? What's the point of the journey? What do I get out of this exhausting climb? And is death the journey's end, or the beginning?

This brings me to my first point . . .

The Unavoidable

You are going to die. (I know. That's a strange way to start a book about life, but stick with me here.) So, at least in this life, we know the journey ends.

No one gets out of here alive. Walk through a cemetery, with rows and rows of tombstones, and you'll see that everyone has that one thing in common. No matter how important that person was, he or she ends up six feet under with a slab of granite on top.

Every tombstone has an end date. Every life has a certain number of breaths that it gets to breathe. Right now, as you read this sentence, you've given up one, maybe two. You don't know when that last one will come, but each one is taking you closer to your journey's end. And the reason that remembering that is the perfect launching pad into a book about life is that it forces us to look intently at the part of the tombstone we don't usually notice. It's the part that lies between the start and end dates: the dash. That's the journey that is your life. You are in your dash right now. And the fact that every dash on every tombstone has a hard stop is what makes this question so urgent: What are you doing with it? What do you want out of your dash?

What Do You Want?

Think about it. What do you want out of life? Where do you hope the journey takes you?

You could be like Anne. She thought how sweet life could be if she had money. At first, it was about how nice it would be to pay the bills without worrying. Then it was about having a lot of nice things, and then the *best* things, and now she has a grade-A, solid-gold stock portfolio that set her up for an amazing retirement, with the leisure time to do all her favorite activities. Skiing in Switzerland. Sun bathing on the Riviera. It's a life others envy, and she knows it. Is that what you want?

Maybe you're like Steve. He went for *power*. He wanted to be the boss. He wanted control. He didn't want to spend his life working for other people's dreams. He wanted other people to work for his. People respected him, even feared him, and it was ideal.

There's also Kim. She was the definition of the phrase *peak physical condition*. No one doubted her sense of personal achievement when it came to her body. And talk about the adrenaline rush she got when she pushed it to the extreme, whether she was cycling or climbing or on the ski runs. You knew from her expression that she felt *alive*. Sound familiar?

I could also talk about Rick, who immersed himself in the greatest sensory experiences he could find. Emotional and physical *snap*, *crackle*, and *pop* is what he wanted.

And on the other end of the spectrum was Jon. He went after enlightenment, striving to hit the pinnacle of knowledge and wisdom.

Will any of these things get you what you really want from life?

Or you might want something more meaningful. You want a relationship where you can love and be loved. You want intimacy, maybe a family. What could be better than being a devoted spouse and a loving parent?

Or maybe it's simply enough for you to make a difference in your world. You want to *matter*. You want to serve and to be recognized for it.

Am I getting close to where your heart is?

You might want all of the above, or maybe you don't even know what you want. But this much is true: *you want something*. Everyone does. It's what gets us out of bed in the morning—even if we can't quite put our finger on it.

SNAPSHOT

KS had it all: power, wealth, fame, health, sex—you name it. He was the rock star of his time. People came from all over the world to spend time with him. He wrote books of philosophy and poetry; he even built one of the most beautiful buildings imaginable. And yet, he declared it all as nothing more than egotistical emptiness. He questioned what mankind ever gained for all of its efforts, since generations pass and the world goes on. "All things are full of weariness," he wrote. We're never satisfied with what we have, and there is nothing new to be done that hasn't been done before. He sought wisdom, he searched for the ultimate pleasures, he accumulated as much wealth as he could, he looked for satisfaction in his work and leisure, in the acclaim he received and in the simplest pleasures, but he still yearned for something else—something that his life couldn't give him. You can read his conclusions in a book called Ecclesiastes.[1]

The Longing

It's sad to think that some people live out their entire lives without ever asking the question, "What do I want?" For them it's too hard. Maybe they're too busy, so the question seems like a luxury. Or maybe they're too let down by life, so to ask is to suffer disappointment, or it might open up a hole that can't be filled. So their "dash" passes like a quiet flash—going nowhere in particular.

There's a problem, though. We can avoid the question, but the *longing* doesn't go away. It's as unavoidable as death. And if we want the most we can get out of life, we have to stop running from it.

You and everybody who ever lived longs for something. You may try to satisfy it with things that ease the longing or go for things that don't work at all—like our friends, Anne, Steve, Kim, and Rick above. Not that there's anything inherently wrong with money, power, or pleasure (in the right time and place and for the right reasons), but the worst fate imaginable is when you get it all and, in the words of Bono, you still haven't found what you're looking for.

So what *are* you looking for?

---

1   KS is King Solomon of Israel (born ca. 990; reigned ca. 962–922 BC). Ecclesiastes, found in the Old Testament of the Bible, is a testimony to the search for meaning found in every generation since the beginning of human thought. The statement "All things are full of weariness" can be found in Ecclesiastes chapter 1, verse 8.

> **SNAPSHOT**
>
> You know someone like Jeff. He was the guy who fired on all cylinders, in academics, in his social life, in his work. Everything he ever wanted to do, he did. The jobs he took were in his sweet spot. The woman he married was the wife of most men's dreams. The kids inherited all of their best attributes: looks, ambition, skills, and talent. Jeff called you one day and wanted to meet up at a local cafe, just to catch up. And you were puzzled when Jeff confessed about the ongoing emptiness he felt. For all he had, he still hadn't found that elusive thing he had been looking for. Maybe he was depressed, just a bad day—you don't know. But when you walked to your car, you had to wonder: *If it's true for a guy like Jeff, then what about the rest of us?*

Driven

If I may be so bold, let's put a name to it: happiness. That's it, in a single word. We are all driven by a desire to find happiness. If we're on a journey, it's the reason we're walking. And this idea is nothing new.

The philosopher Aristotle thought so. He considered happiness the end goal of life and of every action. It's what every human being aspires to have. The Dalai Lama would agree. So would Buddha. And Karl Marx. And Nietzsche. And Muhammad. And Thomas Jefferson. And Epicurus. And John Lennon. And Jesus. And the vast majority of philosophers, prophets, and poets. Though they might differ in explaining how that happiness can be found, they'd all agree that we all want it.

Blaise Pascal, a seventeenth-century French mathematician, said, "All men seek happiness. This is without exception. Whatever different means they employ, they all tend to this end. . . . The will never takes the least step but to this object. This is the motive of every action of every man."[2]

You want to be happy. And not only now, in this minute, but for the rest of the day, the month, the year, throughout your entire life, and beyond! That's why most people throughout history have experienced a shared longing for heaven—the ultimate *happily ever after*.

Most of us work hard to find happiness without even knowing it's what we're looking for. The girl you met online might be the one to make you happy. That guy across the room could be the one. The next big achievement at the office or on the court, the launch of that business, the latest philosophy or self-help guru, that preacher, this new approach—if any of that is attractive, it's because we're attracted to our own happiness. "Please, God," the unconscious prayer of every human heart petitions, "let me find happiness before my dash comes to an end." You may even hope to have it forever.

This is the motive of every action of every human, and to continue Pascal's quote, it's even the motive of "those who hang themselves." Yes, even when our steps are misguided, the thing that keeps us moving anywhere on this journey of life is the hope of arriving at happiness.

SNAPSHOT

AP had come up against a psychological, emotional, and spiritual wall. He was in his thirties, a fairly middle-class young man who had spent a lot of time studying the latest philosophical and moral thinking, debating, and drinking. He even fathered a child by his mistress, and he was tired

---

2   Blaise Pascal, *Pensees Vol. II, Section VII*, translated by W.F. Trotter. (New York: E.P. Dutton & Co., 1958), 113. Originally written in 1660.

of the emptiness he felt. He couldn't change the things he didn't like about himself, and he couldn't find a way to satisfy the nagging feeling that there was more to life than he understood—more to him than he had experienced. The feeling became a physical pain. Did he have the will to pursue all of his questions to their true answers? He wrote that, one day, his "vileness" emerged from the "secret depths of [his] soul" and was piled up in front of him. A "mighty storm arose in [him], bringing a mighty rain of tears." He went off to a garden, flung himself under a tree and felt misery come out of the "bitter sorrow" of his heart. He cried out to the heavens, "How long, how long?" How long would he have to suffer being the unfulfilled and flawed person he knew he was?[3]

The desire for happiness is the foundation of everything you do on this journey of life. It's what you're *really* looking for in your pursuit of [*insert your longing here . . .*].

Recognizing and putting a name to your desire simplifies the journey a bit, doesn't it? But if happiness is the simple hope of every human life, then why are so many people unhappy?

Answering such a complex question seems impossible. But it isn't. There is an answer that can form the foundation for a happy life—even when life is hard, even when you fail at the many things you thought would make you happy, and even when you experience sadness. That one thing is how you see the journey of life itself. That's where faith comes in. Your faith is how you sum up the start date, dash, end date, and the mysterious space beyond the end date. That's the framework for

---

3   AP is Augustine, the son of Patricius (AD 354–430). Born in North Africa, his life fell on the line between the fall of the Roman Empire and the coming Middle Ages. He spent his younger years as a student of philosophy and religion, embracing various schools of thought at the time. Nothing satisfied him. The questions he asked and the answers he found can be read in his classic work *Confessions*. The quotes here come from *Confessions*, Book 8, chapter 12, translated by F.J. Sheed (New York: Sheed & Ward, 1943), 178. I'll talk more about him later.

everything you experience. The question is, Do you have the faith to look for—and find—happiness?

Faith and happiness? Yeah, I know. They seem like mutually exclusive concepts. What does one have to do with the other?

Read on.

Nones

There was a time when people would reach a crisis and turn to religion to find the answers. Or maybe it wasn't a crisis, but it was a time when they asked the ultimate questions about what gives life meaning. They did the party years in college and, when they got jobs, spouses, and kids, they looked for something a little more stable. Sometimes they would return to the church of their childhood.

But things have changed. The fastest-growing religious group in the Western world is the "nones,"[4] the people who don't identify with any particular religion. In the United States, "nones" recently surpassed Roman Catholics as the highest percentage of the population. And more and more people tend to stay nones throughout life.

And yet, more and more people are unhappy.

Generation Z—those born in the middle of the 1990s to the middle of the second decade in the twenty-first century—are the most anxious, most depressed, most despairing generation in history. Studies show that they have lost a sense of purpose and meaning to life. It's no surprise. They may also be the most irreligious generation in history. How's that working for them?

We can pretend all we'd like that the questions that gnaw at every human heart about meaning, what on earth we're here for, and what happens when we die are irrelevant. But those questions have bothered us at our core throughout history,

---

4   See 2018 General Social Survey (by NORC at the University of Chicago), from data collected in 2017, and Pew Research Center surveys conducted December 4–18, 2017.

because we want to be happy, and we need good answers to those questions to achieve happiness. And these can't be just good answers that we made up for ourselves. That would be "make believe," and we know it. We need answers that are *real*.

SNAPSHOT

At the age of seventy-five, Pete Townsend is still trying to figure out who he is. As a founding member of the classic rock band The Who, Townsend created some of the most influential music in rock-and-roll. His musical *Tommy* was a pivot point in rock history. Yet, for all of the fame and acclaim, Townsend could not get a true sense of himself as a human being. In several interviews, he confessed his own confusion and his disillusionment with the unfulfilled promises of the 1960s. He said that his generation hoped to create a sense of community through music, serving the spiritual needs of the audience, but admitted, "It didn't work out that way. We abandoned our parents' church, and we haven't replaced it with anything solid and substantial."[5] He yearned to know, but could not come to any conclusions. Or maybe he didn't like the conclusions he came to.

---

5   David Marchese, "The Who's Pete Townsend Grapples with Rock's Legacy, and His Own Dark Past," *New York Times Magazine*, November 24, 2019.

CHAPTER TWO

THE HUNGER GAME

For every need you have, there is something out there to fill it. If your stomach growls, it's because there's something called "food" to fill it. To have a need that can't be fulfilled would make no sense. If there were no such thing as food, that growling in your stomach would be a mystery, a source of frustration, and possibly the cruelest joke ever played on humans.

We know that every heart longs for happiness. Fulfillment. Life to the full. So, how do we get all that?

We can become rich, famous, and successful, but we all know stories of rich, famous, and successful people who are empty. Take the "27 Club," for instance—the list of actors and musicians who have died from suicide or overdose, all mysteriously at the age of twenty-seven. (Maybe that's about how long it takes to go from leaving your parents' home to the abyss that comes from looking for happiness in all the wrong places.) Jimi Hendrix, Janis Joplin, Jim Morrison, Kurt Cobain, Amy Winehouse—the list is painfully long if you Google it.

Like a child who reacts to hunger by eating a bag of candy, we look to fill the hole with the wrong things. We're relieved for a moment, and in pain afterward. It's worse when we don't realize that the thing we're really hungering for is happiness.

But we don't know how to get it. Is it any surprise when life's journey ends in ruin?

Jim Owens[1]

All of us have appetites in this life, and many of those appetites are met pretty easily. We're hungry, we eat, and we're satisfied. We're thirsty, we drink, and we're satisfied. We want to achieve something, we do it, and we're satisfied. But we also have the sense that all the eating and the drinking, all the productivity in the world, does not satisfy us completely. We have an appetite for something in the very core of our being, which nothing in this world seems to satisfy. What will it take to have lasting happiness? If you knew, would you take it? If you could be happy forever, would you turn that down?

That hole inside of you wants to be filled. We looked at some of the ways you can fill it. But eventually, if you're completely honest, you realize there's something more to be found. If not, then why do so many people with wealth, fame, relationships, power, and influence commit suicide? How could they possibly annihilate themselves when they've achieved the very things a lot of people yearn to have? Why do statistics show that lottery winners often suffer from ruined lives after receiving their money? We see the carnage of wrecked relationships as people move from one to another, in search of that elusive fulfillment. Men and women in peak condition fall into depression when age catches up to them and their bodies no longer provide satisfaction. Every means of happiness we concoct for ourselves eventually reverses itself, or simply fades, or,

---

1   Jim Owens is a professional counselor. His quotes come from interviews for *The Search* video series.

worse, intensifies in a never-ending cycle of need, satisfaction, and greater need.

What do you want? Why are you here? What's your place in the world? Even if you get everything you want, will you be happy?

SNAPSHOT

Jack seemed to have been born with a yearning to know and understand both the world around him and the world within him. He looked up to the best thinkers of his time, and he looked down on all those old-fashioned and outdated ideas and philosophies from the past. Then a war began. He had to march off to another country and fight. He lost friends he loved. He was wounded by a piece of shrapnel that would stay lodged in his chest most of his life. The experience caused him to double-check the merits of modern thinking. He thought about God, but couldn't accept that one existed—and even resented it for not existing. He threw himself into his work, studying literature to become a professor at a prestigious university. Yet, for all of his knowledge and efforts, he could not find the answers to the questions that constantly needled him. He believed they were out there somewhere. They had to be. Otherwise, what was the point?[2]

So, what does it all mean? And how can I possibly be *really* happy without those questions answered?

---

2   Jack is Clive Staples Lewis (1898–1963), a scholar, professor at Oxford and Cambridge, and author of *The Chronicles of Narnia*, *The Screwtape Letters*, and works of science fiction, poetry, and essays. His own account of his search is *Surprised by Joy*.

CHAPTER THREE

WHEN SETBACKS ARE SETUPS FOR COMEBACKS

If you're wondering if you've been looking for happiness in the wrong places, then maybe you have been. Just ask former NBA player and coach Bill Hanzlik.

If you get a chance to sit down with Bill, you get an immediate sense of his exuberance for life. He maintains a warmth and friendliness, even while talking in no-nonsense terms. Playing and coaching in the NBA was a roller-coaster ride for him, but few ever denied that he maintained a burning desire to be the very best, to push beyond his own limitations, even compensating for his height disadvantage by giving all he had to every play.

"I was just the Wisconsin farm boy," Bill says. "I wanted to play basketball. I wanted to be on that court. But there were a lot of great players. How could I get in? I was fortunate enough to try out for the '80 Olympic team. I was one of the last players to make it. Because of that, my dream prospect vaulted from being a third- or fourth-round pick to the first round by the Seattle SuperSonics."[1]

Bill played two years with the SuperSonics and eight with the Denver Nuggets. Three back operations later, he had to change direction. He served as an assistant coach, first with the Charlotte Hornets, and then with the Atlanta Hawks. In

---

1   All quotes from Bill Hanzlik come from his interviews for *The Search* video series.

1997, the Denver Nuggets were looking for a head coach. Bill got the job.

"This was the culmination of my basketball career. I thought, 'Wow, this is unbelievable. I get to coach in the hometown that I love,'" Bill remembers. "As the season started off, I was excited but I knew that my first year was going to be extremely difficult. We weren't going to win a lot of games. Our best player tore his ACL. He was done for the season. We had other players that got hurt. It got even worse. I was playing five rookies. You don't win in the NBA with five rookies."

It was painful for fans to watch. The Nuggets went ten games without a single win. "One stretch we lost 23 straight," Bill admits. "It looked like we may have the worst record ever in the NBA. This was brutal. The media was pounding on me. My family was suffering. Every day, I prayed: 'God, what is your plan for me?' That was the toughest, *toughest* year of my life. I made it through the season. And I thought, 'Okay, this could be a chance to move forward.'"

It wasn't. Bill was fired.

"I was called in the GM's office," Bill recalls. "I walk out with a box of my stuff. I'm thinking, 'What am I going to do now?' My life had been about basketball. I love the sport. And the rug got pulled out from underneath me. 'What's life about now?'"

Sometimes our setbacks push us to the big questions. What's the point of it all? *Is there a point?*

Bill Hanzlik dove deeper into his faith and into service. He started a foundation with a mission "to prepare kids for the game of life." In 1998, they began constructing a facility on fourteen acres of land, completing the Gold Crown Field House in 2003. They have helped almost eighteen thousand kids.

Now he wonders, "What if I got another contract extension? What if I made more money? What if I had won a championship? That would have been really cool. But would it have fulfilled me? So many things don't satisfy our lives. You have to search for the meaning to your life; that's when you're going to find true happiness. The reason why you're here is to search for that meaning. If you search, you will find."

Bill became a man of service, because of his faith. He is one of the happiest men you'll meet. If he had kept succeeding, that wouldn't have been the case. I have to ask: What is success, anyway? Do you know?

What is human existence all about? We want answers, *real* answers, to live a good life, a life of meaning. We want happiness. The answers we're looking for are there. But do you *really* want to know what they are?

Maybe the quest for answers can start by looking in the mirror.

CHAPTER FOUR

YOU

Let's turn our attention from the big picture of life to marvel over the wonder of *you*.

That longing you have for happiness—why is it there? And where is "there" anyway? Your brain? Your "heart"? Your *soul*? What are you?

There are approximately 7.5 billion people on the planet Earth. Put yourself in the middle of a crowd that big, and it'd be easy to feel small. Wanna feel even smaller? The Earth you currently share with that crowd is so minuscule on the grand stage of space that it would take 1,300,000,000 of them to fit inside of our sun. Go further. The Milky Way galaxy is one hundred thousand light years across, and even that's a fairly small galaxy, compared to those that are six *million* light years across. The Hubble telescope has found *fifteen thousand* of those galaxies.

It's daunting to think about it. But we shouldn't confuse smallness with insignificance. You may feel like a tiny speck in the vast cosmos, but that doesn't suggest the cosmos is more significant than you are. On the contrary, you are more significant than any rock, no matter how big it may be.

It's easy to marvel at the mystery of the universe, but stop and consider the mystery of *you*. You share characteristics with the rest of humanity, and yet in the entire history of this planet, there has never been another you. And when you're gone, there will never *be* another you. Not even a God could say he's you. You're the only one who gets to be you.

And the odds of you existing at all are astronomically small. Consider all the balls of gas and rocks floating around in space, the combination of factors that allowed for life to exist on this particular planet, the emergence of humans not only inhabiting the world but learning and developing and inventing over thousands of years—and now, in this time and place, you come along. It's remarkable, if not a miracle.

The Long Chain

Here's a look at just one of the countless improbabilities that paved the way for your existence: Scientists have theorized that, sixty-six million years ago, there was a huge *crack* in the sky, and a seven-and-a-half-mile-wide asteroid shot toward the

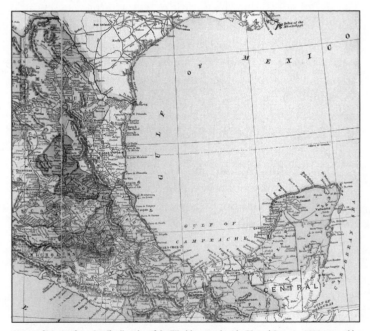

A map of Mexico from Spofford's Atlas of the World, printed in the United States in 1900, created by Rand McNally & Co. © JimPruitt/Shutterstock.com

earth. In time, it struck what we call the Yucatan Peninsula. It was an amazing hit, slamming into a precise point in our world to change everything. Had it hit a few minutes sooner, it would have splashed into the ocean. If it hit a few minutes later, it might have missed the Earth completely. But no, it hit in just the right place to produce enough soot to fill the atmosphere. And because of that soot, the dinosaurs were wiped out. The domino effect allowed for the arrival and evolution of mankind. Imagine the first two humans. They came to exist within a breathtaking margin of error. And yet that asteroid was really set in motion to strike in precisely that place and time from the moment all matter came hurtling into the void 13.8 billion years ago at the big bang. It's as if it was all meant to be. As if you were meant to be. Through almost impossible odds.

Now, consider the margin of error for you to be here. Think of how many things throughout the course of history had to happen in a specific way for you to have your moment on the stage of space and time. If forty thousand years ago a caveman ran *right* instead of *left* to get away from that saber-toothed tiger, he might not have met the cavewoman who was your great-to-the-tenth-power grandma. And you wouldn't be here!

Now imagine this: every decision made by every human at every link of the long chain reaction of life eventually led to you.

From that very first explosion of the universe, you were set in motion.

And as marvelous as the universe is, on a physical, biological level, *you* are even more amazing. You have tens of trillions of living cells in your body, each more rare than all the rocks and balls of gas in the night sky, and each one working, in its own way, more spectacularly than a lifeless star.

Dr. Sean Innerst[1]

The human body is a remarkable thing. Your body is made up of about 37 trillion cells, all with specific functions. Your heart beats 100,000 times per day. Your eyes can distinguish up to 7.5 million different colors. Your fingers can feel a ridge as small as 13 nanometers in size—that's 7,500 times smaller than the diameter of a human hair. If all the DNA in your body were uncoiled, it would stretch out to about 10 billion miles.

But at the center of it all is the crown jewel: your brain. In every way it's been tested, the brain is still far superior to the most powerful computers in existence. A piece of brain tissue the size of a grain of sand contains 100,000 neurons and a billion synapses, all communicating with each other. Brain information travels up to an impressive 268 miles per hour. Your brain can process an image that your eyes have seen for as little as 13 milliseconds, less time than it takes for you to blink. Your brain's storage capacity is considered virtually unlimited and is capable of 10 quadrillion processes per second. Your brain even engages in rewiring itself, a synaptic pruning that deletes the neural connections that are no longer necessary or useful, and then strengthening the necessary ones.

Yet, for the marvel that it is, your ability to think, to reason, and to know—your consciousness—is more than just a biological reality.

---

1   Dr. Sean Innerst is a professor at St. John Vianney Seminar and at the Augustine Institute in Denver. Dr. Innerst's quotes come from interviews for *The Search* video series.

More Than That

Something is definitely going on. You are more than just your body or your brain. The fact that you are thinking about the meaning of your life—of your place in the scheme of things, of more than mere survival—demonstrates that you are not just a lump of self-aware molecules that happened to emerge from the primal sludge.

John Henry Newman

The nineteenth-century essayist John Henry Newman marveled over the workings of the human mind.[2] He wrote that it "ranges to and fro, and spreads out, and advances forward with a quickness which has become a proverb, and a subtlety and versatility which baffle investigation. It passes on from point to point, gaining one by some indication; another on a probability; then availing itself of an association; then falling back on some received law; next seizing on testimony; then committing itself to some popular impression, or some inward instinct, or some obscure memory; and thus it makes progress not unlike a clamberer on a steep cliff, who, by quick eye, prompt hand, and firm foot, ascends how he knows not himself; by personal endowments and by practice, rather than by rule, leaving no track behind him, and unable to teach another. . . . And such mainly is the way in which all men, gifted or not gifted, commonly Reason—not by rule, but by an inward faculty."[3]

---

2   John Henry Newman (1800–1891) would eventually become an Anglican priest, then join the Catholic Church, rising to the role of a cardinal. He was canonized as a saint by the Church in 2019.
3   John Henry Newman, *Sermons, Chiefly on the Theory of Religious Belief,* Preached before the University of Oxford (London: J. G. F. & J. Rivington, 1843), Sermon XII, p. 252.

Every experience of life—from love, to friendship, to what we experience when we look at a beautiful sunset—says to us, "You're more than just a bag of bones and synapses."

Not all think so. A wide range of people, from all professions, have taken a "materialist" view of human beings. They would agree with philosopher of the mind John Searle, who argued that our universe "consists entirely of mindless, meaningless, unfree, non-rational, brute physical particles," with the challenge of reconciling that with our view that we are "conscious, intentionalistic, rational, social, institutional, political, speech-act performing, ethical and free will possessing agents."[4]

George Wald, a Harvard University chemistry professor, put this view in perspective when he quipped that "400 years ago, there was a collection of molecules named Shakespeare, which produced Hamlet."[5] His point wasn't to disparage humans, but to "exalt the molecule."[6] Somehow, though, it still feels as if we've been disparaged.

For Wald, and others like him, the brain is simply "a physical system whose operation is governed solely by the laws of chemistry and physics. What does this mean? It means that all of your thoughts and hopes and dreams and feelings are produced by chemical reactions going on in your head (a sobering thought). The brain's function is to process information. In other words, it is a computer that is made of organic (carbon-based) compounds rather than silicon chips."[7] According to these thinkers, things like meaning and love and

---

4   John Searle, *Freedom and Neurobiology: Reflections on Free Will, Language, and Political Power* (New York: Columbia University Press, 2013), 22.
5   George Wald, "Life in the Universe—From Cosmology to Politics," paper presented at Oak Ridge Bicentennial Lectures: Technology and Society, Oak Ridge, TN, April–October 1976 (Washington, DC: Energy Research and Development Administration, 1977), 25.
6   Wald, "Life in the Universe—From Cosmology to Politics," 25.
7   Leda Cosmides and John Tooby, *Evolutionary Psychology: A Primer* (Santa Barbara: University of California, Center for Evolutionary Psychology, 1997), 4.

thought and aspirations and inspiration and imagination are nothing more than the results of chemical reactions going on in your head. And what we call the soul is merely an extension of the uniquely human workings of the brain, creating an imaginative possibility, or a form of wishful thinking, almost as ridiculous as the idea that we're *made* for happiness, or a place like heaven.

Now we go back to our earlier question: Why feel something that can't be fulfilled? What brutal trick of biology or chemistry would cause us to hope that we are more than all that, or to search for a meaning of life that can't be found? Why would human beings suffer such an ache, when no other creature does? By now, you'd think evolution would have removed such a counterproductive flaw.

But it hasn't. Maybe it isn't a flaw at all. Maybe that longing, when we listen to it, leads us on the ultimate journey—a spiritual journey—that people of all walks of life across all cultures have taken throughout history.

CHAPTER FIVE

THE SOUL

It's interesting to me that the person who prides himself on being too smart for established religion, with its concepts like the soul, often prides himself on being "spiritual" at the same time. Even the atheist who doesn't seem to mind the idea of total annihilation after death sometimes admits a desire for an eternal paradise. Who wouldn't? Maybe that's why the idea has caught on so well throughout history. It's a collective kind of wishful thinking.

Or maybe the idea exists because it is true.

The British have something called "the Blitz Spirit." Early in World War II, the Nazi bombing of civilian populations in England killed or injured more than one hundred thousand people, with many more displaced from their homes. In the thick of it all, the British prided themselves on their ability to carry on with whatever needed to be done. They got up, got dressed, put the kettle on, and went to work. It's inspiring, really. The human spirit rose above terrible circumstances.

Sadly, the end result was that quite a few people accepted their self-sufficiency as evidence that faith didn't have a lot of practical use. So, in many ways, it's no surprise that some of the world's most famous and outspoken atheists are British. It's considered noble in some circles to carry on with life when faced with grim realities, like Nazi bombings, or the concept that you're no more than an assembly of self-aware molecules on a fast track to nothingness. "Chin up, old boy. Get on with it. Make some tea. Head to work. It won't mean anything in the end, but there you are."

Practical, yes. But ultimately, what a disappointment.

Mind if I give you the freedom to hope? Stop for a moment and allow that every childlike desire in your heart for a life beyond this one can actually be fulfilled. The miracle that is you is more than a bag of bones wrapped up in skin with a very smart sponge between the ears to guide it. And I'm not just asking you to hope with me because it's a nice idea, but because there's a growing mountain of evidence that what humanity has always hoped for is *true*.

Fifty Is the New Thirty! And Just Maybe, Death Is the New Birth

At the Fifth Congress of the European Academy of Neurology (EAN) in 2019, researchers presented studies from thirty-five countries showing that one in ten people have had what is commonly called a "near death experience" (NDE). Multiple studies have shown that many who have been declared dead, but have come back, also have *memories* of things they experienced on the other side.[1]

These aren't merely anecdotal stories. Modern medicine has documented hundreds of cases, with a growing number of peer-reviewed clinical studies that point to experiences that cannot be dismissed as fantasy, delusion, or dreams. The people who physically died had unexplainable out-of-body experiences. They saw and heard conversations in the waiting room, far away from where their bodies lay on a gurney. They saw specific images of, for example, a child wearing mismatched clothes who entered the waiting room. One person described seeing a shoe

---

1   Gideon Lichfield, "The Science of Near-Death Experiences: Empirically Investigating Brushes with the Afterlife," *The Atlantic*, April 2015.

sitting on an outside ledge of the hospital, positioned where the patient could never have seen it. More so, she described in great detail what the shoe looked like: a worn toe, a lace resting under the heel. The psychologist who interviewed this patient climbed out onto the ledge and saw it exactly as described. The conclusion? The patient could only have seen the shoe if she had floated *outside* of the window and looked at it closely.[2]

Here's a stranger fact: 80 percent of people who were born blind and had near-death experiences describe being able to see in their experiences. They saw in detail what they could not have imagined.[3]

And most beautifully, many who came back from the other side describe an encounter with an overwhelming love. It's not uncommon for people to describe sadness over having to return.

How is any of that possible if there's not an immaterial part of you—a consciousness—that goes beyond your body? The simple answer is, *it's not*. Turns out, we aren't just material girls (or boys), and we aren't merely living in a material world. (Yes. I realize that I just dated myself by referencing a 1980s song.) There's more.

I believe these facts partially explain the longing we've been talking about. That immaterial part of us is why we human beings have always looked for something more than the things of the material world to make us happy. I'm not claiming those things aren't important. But if you are merely a body, a physical machine, then the only thing that would matter is to keep the machine in good working condition: well rested, well fed, reproducing on a regular basis. And that should be enough. But we all know it's not.

---

2   Douglas M. Stokes, *Reimagining the Soul: Afterlife in the Age of Matter* (Jefferson, NC: McFarland & Co., 2014), 117. Stokes also cites studies by Czech psychiatrist Stanislav Grof (1990) and Mary Roach's *Spook: Science Tackles the Afterlife* (New York: W. W. Norton & Co., 2005), 277.
3   See research by Dr. Kenneth Ring, professor of psychology at the University of Connecticut, and coresearcher Sharon Cooper. Dr. Ring is cofounder of the International Association for Near Death Studies.

There's something different about us, different from all of the other living beings on the planet.

There are no alligators in the swamp wishing they could be movie stars. There are no pigs rolling in the mud yearning to cure cancer. You won't find a single ape, no matter how much it may seem humanlike, pondering the beauty of a Monet. The part of you that wants answers to the question "What is the meaning of life?"—the part of you that desires authentic love, seeks understanding, and questions existence—is something beyond the physical you.

And you know it on a gut level. You always have. That's why the worldview pushed by atheists isn't more popular than it is. Sure, it's growing, for a variety of convoluted reasons that have more to do with fashion than actual thought. It's received the backing of some in academia and pop culture. But those who believe in the soul and an afterlife remain a vast majority in the world.

Frankly, the idea that we're here just to die doesn't fit our experience of life, or of ourselves, or of our hope for the future. That's because of what author G. K. Chesterton called our "instinct for the probable."[4] The fact that we are a combination of the material and the immaterial, a unique body-soul miracle that stands out from the whole universe, isn't merely wishful thinking. It's the most *probable* thing.

And the great news about the longing deep in our souls for real meaning, real life, real joy, real love, and real happiness—and not just small amounts, but infinite amounts—is because that longing has an answer. Hope with me. I dare you.

Author C. S. Lewis noted that if we find ourselves with a desire that nothing in *this* world can satisfy, then the most probable explanation is that we're made for *another* world.[5]

---

4   G. K. Chesterton, *The Everlasting Man* (1925; repr., San Francisco: Ignatius Press, 2008), 50.
5   C. S. Lewis, *Mere Christianity* (London: Geoffrey Bles, 1952), 108.

Dr. Sean Innerst[6]

So, where does the soul come from? Strictly speaking, a mother and father can only contribute our body to us, the physical part of us. In order to be the human beings we know we are—more than a collection of self-aware molecules— we have to be immediately in-souled by something or someone outside of us. There are many religious theories about this, but it's the Judeo-Christian tradition that makes it clear. An account in the book of Genesis in the Bible states that the soul is made in the image and likeness of God, who, in the poetic language of the Bible, breathed life into the nostrils of the dust that was Adam (Gen 2:7). As a result, we—unlike any other creature—are capable of knowing and choosing freely. And that's what makes us specifically human. It's something that comes directly from God as an expression of his own image, as a supremely rational and loving being. And so, inside each and every human soul, there is an imprint of God's own capacity to know and love.

You're a Big Deal

Compared to the vastness of the universe, you may feel small— and physically you are. But spiritually you're a big deal. You are more significant than any galaxy, any mountain range, any ocean. They will all disappear, but you won't—because your God-infused soul is eternal. And you're made in the image and likeness of God. You can know. You can love. You can make choices. Quasars and oceans and galaxies and flowers can't do that—only you.

Many authors and theologians have pondered the moment when Adam first laid eyes on Eve—and what it was like for

---

6   Dr. Innerst's quotes come from interviews for *The Search* video series.

him when he first saw her, her feet gently touching on the earth beneath her, yet with an inner power that towered over the mountain behind her, and a light in her eyes that shone brighter than anything he had seen—intelligence, wonder, free will, the capacity to love him. He may have mistaken her for a deity. Yet she was no more than you.

Religion isn't just rooted in the idea that God is amazing. It's rooted in the idea that we are. Why else should we dare to dream of a heaven, or that the God who put this longing-filled soul in us would have a plan to fulfill every longing, or that he'd even notice us in the massive universe?

Sound crazy? If so, then it's a craziness that has united human beings from the beginning of time. We humans aren't just vaguely spiritual; we're profoundly religious. If you go to distant, untouched jungles, you will find people who have created rituals to give expression to a deep yearning to connect with something beyond themselves.

Go to Israel and you'll see a temple, a place Jews used for centuries as their place of worship. In the center of that temple is an altar, which served as a connecting point to God.

Every Catholic Church in the world has an altar.

Go to Greece and Rome and you'll see the ancient altars where they offered sacrifice to their gods.

Zoom to the other side of the planet in Hawaii and you'll find *heiau*—the Hawaiian word for temples. In those, you'll find *ahu*, the altar.

There are altars in these different cultures in different parts of the world that never had any form of communication with each other. Why do they reach out to an unseen someone or something in an act of worship? Were they borne out of a collective ignorance, or were they doing what you're doing right now: searching? They, like us, looked around—or rather, looked up—and asked the most natural and human questions ever: Where did the world come from? What is my place in it?

How do I honor or appease the source of everything I see and all that I am? What can I give back?

They wanted to give outward expression to their inward longing—the longing of all of mankind.

St. Augustine

Question the beautiful earth; question the beautiful sea; question the beautiful air, diffused and spread abroad; question the beautiful heavens; question the arrangement of the constellations; question the sun brightening the day by its effulgence; question the moon, tempering by its splendor the darkness of the ensuing night; question the living creatures that move about in the water, those that remain on land, and those that flit through the air, their souls hidden but their bodies in view, visible things which are to be ruled and invisible spirits doing the ruling; question all these things and all will answer: "Behold and see! We are beautiful." Their beauty is their acknowldgement.[7]

---

7   St. Augustine, *Sermons On The Liturgical Season*, translated by Sister Mary Sarah Muldowney, R.S.M. (New York: Fathers Of The Church, Inc., 1959), 256

CHAPTER SIX

GOD

Without an author, there's no story. Without an artist, there's no painting. Both give a shape and meaning to their work that comes only from them.

Without a God, we have to concede that there's no ultimate meaning to life, other than what we make up, which, as we know, would only be "make believe." To have ultimate happiness, we need real answers to life's ultimate questions. We need to know that life has meaning—*real* meaning. And to have that, we need something outside of ourselves. We need a God.

That's the conclusion people have made throughout history. In their desire to be happy, they have believed in a God, or many gods, or some amorphous force that resembles God.

But we have to ask: Is there a God? A lot of people think not. Why? What are some of the obstacles to having faith in a God?

Isn't the Idea of God a Kind of Silly, Antiquated Idea?

There was a famous Soviet Russian cosmonaut, an avowed atheist, who went into outer space. Out in the black expanse of the universe, he looked around and declared that he could not see God anywhere. It's a funny thing to have said—and it may have been exactly what his fellow Soviet Russians on earth wanted to hear.

But really, it's like Frodo reaching the peak of Mount Doom and complaining that he looked everywhere but couldn't find J. R. R. Tolkien. If you're in the book, there's an author. If you're in a building, even if you can't see one, there's an architect. If you find yourself in creation, it's safe to say there's a Creator. We call the Creator *God*.

No, God is not a "flying spaghetti monster."[1] He's not a Bronze Age myth atop Mount Olympus either. And he's not a mighty creature flying around in space and time. (Space and time are, in a sense, flying around God.[2]) The God we believe in is existence itself, and like the sun is the source of all our light and heat, he's the source of all that is.

Dr. Liz Klein[3]

I think that people sometimes reject God because they have a false understanding of who and what God is. Even religious people admit that, in the back of their minds, they think of God as this old man in the sky, like Michelangelo's rendering on the roof of the Sistine Chapel. Or, to another extreme, people have this idea of God as a stern judge. Or God might be a nebulous, impersonal force to make sure that the world goes in the right direction. Or God is a non-specific idea, something vague and unapproachable. Or maybe God is like a cruel scientist studying us like rats in a maze. Usually, when people reject God, they're rejecting a false god.

---

1 The "flying spaghetti monster" originated in a 2005 letter from Oregon State University physics graduate and activist Bobby Henderson to the Kansas State Board of Education, protesting its decision to allow intelligent design to be taught as an alternative to the theory of evolution. It later became the god of "Pastafarianism," a satirical religion by those who agreed with Henderson.
2 In line with the Greek philosophers of his time, St. Paul wrote: "In him we live and move and have our being" (Acts 17:28).
3 Elizabeth Klein, PhD, is assistant professor of theology at the Augustine Institute in Denver. Dr. Klein's quotes come from interviews for *The Search* video series.

A lot of people will tell you that man has evolved beyond the need for any kind of God, even if there is one.

Some people argue that faith in God is no more than wishful thinking for those who can't accept reality—just as the belief in an afterlife is simply a coping mechanism, a vain hope, to console us in the face of death. They argue that the fact that we want to believe disproves belief. (I'd argue that it's just another sign that we're made for the stuff we hope for and believe in. But stick with me.) Or maybe the concept of God is a primitive remnant in our brains, like a tail or an appendix in our bodies. And yet, many of those same people will acknowledge that we, as human beings, are "spiritual" in some way. Maybe our "spirits" connect to the cosmos, or to Mother Nature, or to the Force. People who don't believe in faith will often believe in anything.

What Is It?

What do you think of God? Is God a Force above and beyond us, like that neutral entity of energy in *Star Wars*—something benign, a tool to be used like a kind of spiritual hammer? Or maybe God is an entity that created our world, set it into motion, then moved on to other realms, forgetting us completely, as Mark Twain depicted in *Letters from the Earth*. God might be a controlling and manipulative entity, like the power-player in the movie *The Truman Show*. How about a diabolical computer-driven entity as we see in *The Matrix*—a tyrant, a dictator, something that keeps pulling the wool over our eyes to keep us from seeing "reality"? Or God could be like a cruel scientist who watches us run like rats in a maze, maybe hitting us with something nasty just to see how we'll react.

Or maybe God is the One who created us out of love. Is that so hard to accept?

I was once talking with someone who claimed not to believe in God. She had been raised Catholic, but had long ago dismissed the faith handed down through her Italian family for two thousand years. In the course of the conversation, she said, "The Universe is looking out for me." I broke the news to her that if by "the Universe" she meant an intelligent, and therefore personal, cosmic force who ties everything together and cares for and looks out for people, then that's what Catholics mean by the word "God."

Hasn't Science Disproven God?

Good question. I'm glad you asked.

Some argue that if something can't be proven using the "scientific method," it's not real. I need to call that out for what it is. There's a philosophy called "scientism" that many buy in to, even though they know very little about it. Frankly, it's a weak view of the world, since you can't actually use the "scientific method" to prove its validity. See the problem there? And the result of this philosophy is a very boring, very narrow experience of life. Beauty. Goodness. Literature. Love. Right and wrong. Friendship. None of the things that make life amazing are deemed worthy, because they can't be examined in a petri dish. I am not making this up.

William Provine, the late Cornell University historian of science, wrote:

> Modern science directly implies that the world is organized strictly in accordance with mechanistic principles. There are no purposive principles whatsoever in nature. There are no gods and no designing forces that are rationally detectable. . . . Modern science directly implies that there are no inherent moral or ethical laws, no absolute guiding principles for human society. We must conclude that when we die, we die, and that is the

end of us . . . There is no hope of life everlasting. . . . There is no ultimate meaning for humans.[4]

And thus saith scientism.

Apparently, educated people have dispensed with a need for a supreme spiritual being. The only way for mankind to achieve its true potential is to get rid of all these antiquated, religious ideas. Faith and science are antithetical to one another. Right?

If that's true, then someone needs to explain it to Fr. Paul Mueller and Fr. Paul Gabor. They run a cutting-edge, Vatican-owned observatory in the Arizona desert. Fr. Mueller is the first to explain what they're doing on Mount Graham: "Often when people come to visit, the first thing they ask is why the Vatican has an observatory. My reply is that it's because we can't afford a particle accelerator."[5]

Imagine a rim-shot here—thanks.

Anna Wetterer-Nelson[6]

There's a quote I love that says if science is my fingers, faith is my thumb. And between the two of them, I can grasp anything. The fact that we're able to witness what science has discovered, to see even at the microscopic level the patterns and symmetry and beauty, is astonishing. The more I look, the harder it is for me to believe that there isn't a higher power governing what we know. The more I learn and have discovered about the universe, the more sure I am about my faith.

---

4   William Provine, "Evolution and The Foundation of Ethics," *MBL Science 3*, no. 1 (Winter 1988), 25–29.
5   Fr. Meuller's and Fr. Gabor's quotes come from interviews for *The Search* video series.
6   Anna Wetterer-Nelson is a computer-science teacher at Cherry Creek High School in Denver, Colorado. Anna Wetterer-Nelson's quotes come from interviews for *The Search* video series.

If faith and science are antithetical, then Georges Lemaître should have been told. He's the man who came up with the Big Bang Theory. He was a man of faith. And there's Roger Bacon, the grandfather of the scientific method most commonly used now. He would be very surprised. He was a man of faith. Both, in fact, were Catholic priests.

Nicholas Copernicus, the pioneer of Heliocentrism, and Jean-Baptiste Lamarck, who prefigured the theory of evolution, and Gregor Mendel, the friar who advocated a theory of genetics, were all people of faith. So was Fr. Angelo Seki, the father of stellar spectroscopy.

Thirty-five lunar features on the moon were named after the priests who had discovered them.

Historically, science wasn't an effort to disprove God's role in the world, but to better understand the world God had created. And despite some recent bad branding, people of biblical faith were driven to the physical sciences not in spite of their worldview, but because of it.

They believed in a mastermind behind the world because they saw an order to creation. Unlike the pagans, they believed that God was separate from the world—so it was okay to poke, prod, and dissect things, because it wouldn't upset the flower nymph, volcano god, water fairies, or tree of souls. Have at it! Explore what God has created.

As Fr. Mueller notes, "You can't even do science unless you start with the presupposition that the world itself is stable and reasonable and orderly. Science can't prove that the world is going to be the way tomorrow that it is today. Science can't prove that we can make sense of reality. Science has to *presuppose* that."

Ever wonder why some of the most brilliant scientists in history arose from Catholic countries in Europe over the past millennia? Do you know that the Church invented the university system in Europe? Ever wonder why the natural sciences thrived in Christian culture throughout history? It's because the science-versus-faith narrative of history simply isn't true. Even when the Church and science appeared to collide, the Church was not acting from an anti-science position, but often from the prevailing view of science itself at the time.

Dr. Karin Öberg[7]

I'm combining my expertise in chemistry and astronomy to try to figure out how our solar system formed, how our Earth became habitable as the living planet it is, how other planets form, and the likelihood of finding other living planets out there. I actually find that modern cosmology is telling us something about the personality of the Creator. I mean, this seems to be a God who wants the universe to participate in creating, where we see how the universe changes over time, and new structures—often with unexpected structures—appear, but still in accordance with the laws of nature. Because the world exists at all points to that, I believe a Creator created the world. I think the beauty of the cosmos points toward a Creator that is beautiful, and values beauty. The intelligibility of the world points to an intelligent Creator.

The Limitations of Unlimited Science

Modern science has done a great job. (Go, science!) It has helped us understand what sort of creatures we are, how our various parts work, where we came from. But the very success

---

7   Dr. Karin Öberg is a professor of astronomy at Harvard University. Dr. Orberg's quotes come from interviews for *The Search* video series.

of modern science can tempt us to believe that its questions are the only questions, its answers the only answers, and that there is no more to say about us or the world than what it can say. Since the infancy of modern science, certain thinkers and writers have succumbed to this temptation and taken it upon themselves to tell us that science is the whole truth—complete and irrefutable—about us. But we all know that's not true—simply by our experience of life.

It's been said that faith and reason are like two wings on the back of the human spirit, allowing it to rise high in its contemplations and explorations to know and understand itself and everything around it.[8]

It is wired into the human heart to do the very thing we're doing now: ask questions and seek out the truth—the *whole* truth.

Science can only view or measure those things that can be viewed or measured. Science doesn't work with anything it can't see, hear, touch, or comprehend as physical fact. Science can dissect a body and identify the parts, but it can't explain the meaning of a person or his life. The full picture of reality is more than science can give us. Faith, on the other hand, can do what science can't: open our minds to the fullness of truth.

Dr. Liz Klein[9]

Scientism is a kind of scientific fundamentalism, much in the way you have biblical fundamentalism among certain Christian groups. Biblical fundamentalism is a way of seeing

---

8   See Pope John Paul II, encyclical letter *Fides et Ratio*, September 14, 1998, http://www.vatican.va/content/john-paul-ii/en/encyclicals/documents/hf_jp-ii_enc_14091998_fides-et-ratio.html.

9   Dr. Klein's quotes come from interviews for *The Search* video series.

the world through a strict, but limited, understanding of the Bible—concluding that anything you ever need to know about everything is stated there plainly by God. Likewise, scientism states that science can tell us everything we ever need to know or hope to discover about the universe—and if it can't, then it's not worth knowing.

The natural sciences take, as a starting point, only what can be seen and learned from the world. Theology, in contrast, studies something that, by definition, is transcendent, above space and time, above the physical universe. So they are two different disciplines that overlap, but they don't have to conflict.

Listen to Creation

So, back to the big question, which is arguably the biggest of the big questions: Is there a God? While the scientific realm can't prove or disprove the existence of God, it seems that the more we learn about the world all around us, the more it shouts to us about the existence of a Maker.

We used to think the universe was expanding very rapidly through space and time. We know better now. The universe is not expanding through space and time, because the universe contains space and time. Think about that. If you wanted to step "outside" the universe, there is no "out there" to step into. So we have to ask, "Where did the Big Bang happen?" The answer is simply that, before the Big Bang, there was no "where." Then we have to ask, "When did it happen and how long was there nothingness before it happened?" The answer, again, is that there was no "how long," because there was no such thing as time.

And then all of a sudden, there was an explosion, and 13.8 billion years later rational creatures are walking around drinking lattes. You want me to believe that a Maker has nothing to do with that? I think that would take more of a "leap of faith" than faith in God does.

We all know that nothing can't do something. It certainly can't cause an explosion that results in everything. Every material *thing* had to be made by some material *thing*. It would be insane of me to presume the laptop I'm now using spontaneously appeared on my lap, unless you saw another species like me with laptops mutating from their thighs. But we'd think it was ridiculous for the laptop or my thighs or *me* to come from nothing.

The universe is a thing, just like my laptop. It's an unimaginably huge material thing, in fact. But like any other material thing, it has parameters to it—edges. It's finite. And like any other thing, it must have a source—a cause. We call that cause God.

"Wait," you say, "doesn't God also need a cause?" Nope. The things we're talking about are material things—made of "stuff" or of "matter." God is not material. He doesn't need a "Genesis." It works for a material thing to come from an immaterial thing, but not for a material thing to come from nothing. Nothing does not have the power to become something. However, a pre-existing God who is immaterial can certainly have the power to make a material universe.

Atheists who say, "You don't know the answer, so you insert God into the equation," call him the "God of the gaps." But those same people ask us to insert a "science of the gaps" into the missing parts of their theories. They claim that we must have faith that they'll one day figure it out through a purely natural explanation. Place your bets, then, on what faith you'll need for what conclusion. And even then, we'll have to ask what caused the cause they come up with.

Can I explain how or why there was a God instead of nothing? No. All I know is that, because there's something, there's God. And I also know that it's not so much an act of faith as it is an act of thinking. This is why most of the great minds throughout history—from the ancient philosophers to Einstein, to many scientists now—have believed in a Creator. As Einstein said, "I want to know God's thoughts; the rest are details."[10]

But even those who claim to believe only in science are believers, in some sense. Ironically, as we've already noted, the foundation of scientific knowledge is the assumption that the world has a certain intelligibility to it—that it has order and consistency and beauty that we can make sense of, learn from, and respond to.

Many scientists concede the need for a "leap of faith" in any scientific theory. We know that the atom exists because evidence points to manifestations of the atom, but we have never seen an atom. Evolutionary theory can only go so far in its explanations about the development of humans, but there is then a much-needed leap to connect those explanations to other explanations.

Like anyone else, they have their own framework or truths that seem self-evident to them and within which they perceive everything.

Doesn't the Big Bang Theory or the Theory of Evolution Conflict with the Bible?

In the words of theologian and author Dr. Edward Sri, "We need to make sure we approach the Bible, or any piece of literature, by asking what the author intended to communicate . . . in its original historical context, while considering the literary genres and the modes of expression that are being used."[11]

---

10   The quotation is from Esther Salaman, "A Talk with Einstein," *The Listener* 54 (1955), 370–71.

11   Dr. Sri's quotes come from interviews for *The Search* video series.

To put it simply, the author of Genesis wasn't writing a scientific history. The audience, thousands of years ago, wouldn't have cared. Nor do most people today. I personally enjoy geeking out on astrophysics, but most people don't. The author was conveying what happened to get to the heart of where it all began and what it all means. Like Einstein, he wasn't concerned about the details in a scientific sense, but he wanted to express "God's thoughts."

I realize I've touched just the tip of the iceberg when it comes to some of these questions. I can't do much more than that here. I hope I've given you a few answers to some common objections. Or at least that I've shown that believers aren't non-thinkers. But even these answers—as factual as they are—aren't the same as faith, any more than facts about a beloved spouse can equal a marriage.

Now we have to turn to faith itself. Are you ready?

CHAPTER SEVEN

KNOWING IS HALF THE BATTLE

My mother-in-law, Sylvia, was up late talking to her brother-in-law, Ed. She was trying to convince him about the existence of God. Their conversation stretched into the night. "If God picked up this table in front of me," he conceded, "then I'd believe in him." A minute later he chuckled, "Actually, I probably still wouldn't believe in him!"[1]

As good as our reasons are for faith, and as important as it is to explore every question under the sun, we can't study our way into belief. Belief, like disbelief, isn't just a head game. That's because the end game here isn't a topic. It's not a class you pass or fail. It's a relationship with a Person. It's like marriage. A man meets a woman and she can fulfill every check on his list, but it takes more than things "making sense" to make a marriage. As important as the reasons are, eventually his *will* has to push his intellect beyond where it can go on its own. Then he produces a ring and asks the question, "Will you marry me?"

The same is true with faith. I can present good reasons to believe that there is a God and even state that he has a specific name. Those reasons are important. But at the end of the day, they're not enough. Reasons only bring us to the threshold of faith. And even if we had tangible evidence, like a levitating table, we'd still have to choose to walk over that threshold.

---

1   Ed lived and died without faith. And he hung himself on his sixty-fifth birthday.

But Isn't Faith Unreasonable (and Doesn't That Make It Just a Little Bit Stupid)?

"Unreasonable" and "beyond your ability to reason" aren't the same thing. And faith in things you can't fully grasp is far from unreasonable.

The truth is, we use all kinds of "faith" every day, even though we don't call it that. There are a lot of things we haven't seen for ourselves, can't definitively prove, or don't fully comprehend, yet we accept them to be true. Think about it. How many of us have ever been to the Fiji Islands? Yet, even if we haven't, we believe they exist somewhere in the South Pacific. Why? Because we have faith in the people who have conveyed this information to us. Almost everything we learn in school, from science to history to geography, we take on faith. Even when we cannot immediately prove the truth of what we are learning, we still believe it, partly because it seems plausible and partly because we trust the people who are teaching us.

That base level of trust makes perfect sense. We need it to function. My kids have faith that I didn't poison their school lunches today. They have faith that their school uniforms won't dissolve in the rain. They have faith that their bus driver will take them to school and not to another state. They can't prove any of that, but they have faith none of those things will happen. A combination of experience and trust has formed their expectations. Otherwise, they'd be paranoid and miserable.

The same is true with the most important stuff of life, relationships, and religious faith, none of which can be "proven" in the scientific sense, but all of which we need in order to function.

But How Do We Know Things We Can't Prove?

Faith isn't trusting things that don't make sense. It's opening your heart and mind to things you can't fully make sense of. For example, *2+2 = Turnip* doesn't make sense, and you'd be foolish to believe it. But there are plenty of things that do make sense that you can't fully take in, yet you accept them anyway. You probably don't doubt the existence of the atom, even though you have never actually seen one. In fact, no one has.

Going back to our marriage analogy: Even if a man studied his beloved for years, there would still be so much unknown about her, about their life together, and about the unforeseen changes they'll face in the future. Yet every time a couple approaches the altar to give their lives to each other in marriage, they're saying yes to something that makes sense, but that they can't fully take in. At the very core of marriage may be found the answer to our very first question about finding meaning: Two people make a choice to marry because they want to find meaning. Together they will find happiness. They know their love is real because they believe it, they see hints of it, even though it can't be proven like 2 + 2 = 4. Faith is believing without fully knowing.

Imagine the person who will not accept friendship or love because she can't "prove it," even though it makes perfect sense. Imagine a life spent withholding her trust and her heart. It's the most isolating, empty, and lonely thing. Most people would consider it a disorder of the heart on the highest level.

Dr. Sean Innerst[2]

Sometimes people get impatient with religious teachings because they think they're too complicated. Ironically, they're often tolerant when scientific explanations of material things are so complicated that they can't understand them. It's okay for science to be more complicated; we expect that. But we want our religion kept simple. It's something of a paradox that, when it comes to religion, what is complicated to explain is actually simple in practical application.

Scholar Frank Sheed once used the example of the operation of human respiration—the way the lungs work. It's a very complicated thing. But breathing is simple. That's how it is with religion. On one level it is high and majestic and complex, even hard to explain. And yet, it is really quite simple. Religious people often live simpler and less complicated lives because their focus is clear. They have a focused direction that gives their lives a certain unity and purpose and meaning. Ask them to explain it theologically, and they may not be able to do it. That's the paradox.

Follow the Bread Crumbs

Imagine a child lost in the woods. This child has never been deep in the woods before and has no skills for figuring out how to get out. The child wanders aimlessly, but eventually comes upon a piece of store-bought bread. Then, looking around, the child sees another piece of bread up ahead. Every few yards, the child finds another, leading the child in a particular direction.

2   Dr. Innerst's quotes are from interviews for *The Search* video series.

What might that child reasonably think? One option would be to think: "The bread spontaneously grew here, in that shape, like a fungus." But that would be silly.

If the child is an average, rational kid, he'll probably think: "Bread is something *people* eat. So, this trail of bread might have been dropped by someone and could lead me to people." With nothing more than that, the child may rush forward in faith, hoping the bread will lead to people and, finally, rescue.

Putting the story of Hansel and Gretel aside for a moment, the analogy is simply this: We are lost in the woods, and we're hungry. We're all searching for something that will nourish us and lead us home, and clues have been left that give us every good reason to hope we will find this. Some of us are like the child who looks skeptically at the bread and the trail and stays lost in the woods. Faith is the decision to move forward toward hope.

Who Left the Breadcrumbs?

I'll answer simply: God has.

But who is this God? If we've sensibly rejected the notion that God is some kind of fuzzy old dude in the sky, or that he's a magical being floating on the clouds, or that he's some variation of a superhuman amped up on doses of divinity (that would be the Greek gods, and like us, they were kind of jerks), then we're taking a step in the right direction to know who the true God really is.

To help you understand the true God, I'll have to tell you a story. But before I do that, I'll ask you to take something on faith: *the true God is worth searching for.* Will you accept that much from me? This God is worth knowing. Yes, he can be a little terrifying. It's a little scary to start pursuing someone who isn't old, who doesn't even exist in time, who isn't big, because he transcends everything. But that's the kind of God we're going to meet. That's the kind of God that we want to know more about. Because that's actually an encounter with the meaning of life and the meaning of who we are and the meaning of the universe.

Wanna know all that? Wanna *live* all that? Then you have to go to the source. It's up to you.

Faith in God is a choice. I say it's a reasonable choice. But let me go a step further here. If you want a meaningful life, if you want joy and peace and happiness and a sense of purpose, it's also a *necessary* choice.

And So . . .

Here's what I'm saying. Human beings are not a random accident spawned by a random universe. They are uniquely created in the very image of their Creator. They have intelligence and reason with the will to make choices. They have been hardwired by their Creator to have a desire for something that can't be satisfied by anything the material world has to offer. They actually yearn for something *outside* of the material world because they are more than material beings—they are also spiritual beings that will exist long after their physical bodies have become dust. Instinctively, they want happiness, if we allow that "happiness" means more than simply experiencing pleasure or being content in the moment, but involves a sense of meaning and purpose.

It would be easy to stop here. Many people do. Going forward has the potential to disrupt your life. The noises that drown out the answers are too loud, too entertaining, too hard to resist. The devices we've invented are too distracting. Why bother to climb a mountain when you're surrounded by experts who've said that the mountain isn't necessary; the answers are right here in what you've been told since you were a baby, in what you feel, in what you own. Forget the longing; forget the search. Stop now before it's too late.

Or you can continue on.

It's your choice.

CHAPTER EIGHT

A STORY

Let's shift from logical argument to literature. Everybody loves a good story. It's easy to imagine the earliest humans sitting around the fire, telling stories of the day's hunt, or recounting the legends of great heroes or that thing that lurks in the shadows of the forest. Archeologists have found drawings on cave walls, each telling a story. They were a foreshadowing of painting and stained glass windows and eventually photography and motion pictures.

We love stories because some part of us recognizes that we are in a story of our own. Each one of us could say, "Once upon a time, *I* . . . ," because our lives are our stories, set against a backdrop of a bigger story. Each one of us is like the actor who walked on stage at some point in a very, very long play. This is our scene. You could say that this is our moment in the movie. It's our chapter in an epic novel, one that we didn't create, with a reality that existed before we got here and will continue after we're dead, and yet . . . here we are.

Think about it. From the time you were born, the unique parents you have, where you went to school, the friends that forged who you are today, the good and the bad things that happened, the dreams that are specifically yours, your jobs, career, spouse, kids, whatever it is that makes up your life— they're all part of your story.

Jonathan Pageau[1]

I'm an artist and icon carver, which means that I make icons within the Christian tradition. Because I'm interested in art and iconography, I'm also someone who writes and speaks about symbolism—and about patterns in the world and how the world lays itself out for us.

We are in a very particular moment right now. The history of what happened to the West is quite long, bringing us through a period called the Enlightenment, which took us away from storytelling as a major mode of human experience. We developed a type of rational thinking that led to amazing scientific discoveries. But it led to a kind of thinking that is alienating us. You don't live inside scientific theories. You live in this body, with this experience of the world that lays itself out to you with your five senses, and you engage the world. The experience of sunlight on your face is not the same thing as knowing at what temperature the sun burns.

As an artist, I have to represent reality. I have to represent something. So, if I'm making a painting, or a carving of a person, I cannot represent all the details of that person. They're seemingly infinite. There's an indefinite amount of details, such as every single reflection on every hair, on every pore in your skin. And so I have to make choices about what I'm going to select, in order to make you see a person. By doing that, I'm kind of showing how things come together.

We always tell a story with a purpose. If I take a grocery list, and I read the grocery list, you will know that that's

---

1   Jonathan Pageau is an iconographic artist. His quotes are taken from interviews in *The Search* video series.

not a story. A story is a set of glasses by which I can look at the indefinite potential that is laid out in front of me, so that I can make sense of it. The story of your life has a coherence, like a song, like a poem, that we can enter into and we can dance with. You can't dance to science. It's very good for making cell phones and cars, but our story is a gigantic symphony that we can dive into.

Story 101

Go back to what you learned in English class. Think about what we traditionally mean by "story." A definition might go something like this: a story is an ordered sequence of events, with a beginning, a middle, and an end, in which a protagonist pursues a goal and, after a series of progressive complications (that is, conflicts), either succeeds or fails in attaining the goal, by his or her own efforts, and not by chance but intention. (*Phew!* I never actually thought I'd have to repeat all that after I graduated.)

There you have it: protagonist and conflict. And do you remember your list of conflicts from that English class? There is man versus man, man versus nature, man versus himself, and man versus God.

Now, let's think about your story.

What Are You?

Are you the protagonist? In case you aren't sure, the classic definition of a protagonist is that he or she is simply the chief actor or main character of a story. The . . . roots of this word comes . . . from ancient Greece. There, "protagonist" literally means "first competitor," which implies that a story essentially is a challenge, a trial, in which a character is put to the test. Usually that test is the protagonist trying to get something he or she really wants—and trying to overcome all the obstacles to getting it. In essence, the protagonist is trying to attain a kind of goal.

The best stories show us what the protagonist wants, but then create situations that make it harder and harder for the protagonist to get it. It's a progressive build, with each obstacle becoming harder to overcome. Why? Well, if it's too easy, then we wouldn't have much of a conflict and, without conflict, you don't have much of a story. Romeo wants Juliet. How far will he go to get her? Will Frodo leave the Shire? Will Scrooge die a miserable death? Will Luke Skywalker leave his home planet and join the Resistance to destroy the Death Star? Eventually, all decisions drive the protagonist to a point where the ultimate decision is made—a point of no return—which will change *everything*, for better or worse.

Are you the protagonist in your story? If so, then what do you want—and just what are you willing to risk to get it?

You may be thinking there's nothing you want *that* much. You really don't have a clear, overriding goal. Maybe you have a lot of goals, a variety of things you seem to be pursuing every day. But we covered that at the beginning. There's a through-line to what drives you. We called it "happiness"—or "fulfillment" or "meaning." And whether you realize it or not, you spend a lot of your life pursuing it, just like a protagonist would.

As the protagonist in your story, what you want also comes with obstacles and conflicts. You are living out a full dramatic arc that is called a "plotline." Plotlines are simply the action— the cause and effect of decisions, the setbacks and the steps forward. Stories structure them in a way that makes sense as they unfold and that ultimately builds to a climax.

Setbacks
Think about the obstacles in your story. Your childhood and adolescence, your relationships with parents and siblings and

friends and coworkers, your education, your employment, your successes, your defeats, your sins as well as your acts of goodness, your illnesses, your despair, your marriage, your parenting, your business, political, or social setbacks. You have obstacles in your life, both self-made and outside of your control. And all the while, the goal is always there. You may not pursue it successfully. You've made decisions that have distracted you, made you unhappy, thrown you off the track. You've stopped—maybe for long stretches, for a variety of reasons—and even those things are obstacles.

Maybe the obstacle came in the form of an antagonist. By definition, an antagonist is a person or force in a story that actively works against the protagonist's efforts. It may be someone or something that persistently and purposefully gets in the way.

Whatever the obstacles have been, the plotline pushes on, because life pushes on. You are still in your story, whether you want to be or not.

You Are Not Alone

Your story is not the only story. Have you ever considered the possibility that you're also a secondary character or a walk-on in someone else's story? Those people you went to school with. That coworker or neighbor who came and went years ago. A person from the store or coffee shop that you saw from time to time. A doctor or dentist you've visited. That stranger you helped on the side of the road.

Or maybe you were the antagonist in that other story, working against the goals and desires of the protagonist.

It boggles the mind to think about it. Millions and millions of stories are playing out, many intertwining or colliding. There are stories from the past that have impacted your story, even before yours began. Your story may impact stories that have yet to be told.

One thing you know for sure: your story didn't really begin when you were born. The story of your parents and their parents, of the place you were born and where you spent your formative years, of the state of the country you were in—all affect your story.

Now, at this point, if your story was being told as a film, we might go to a flashback to help put you in that greater context. Your story is big, but there's a much bigger story to be told—and it gives meaning to your story, and everyone else's too.

CHAPTER NINE

FLASHBACK

Your story is part of a story that reaches back before time itself began. Pause for a moment and consider the possibility that every part of your life—every decision, every joy, every pain, every detail in the plotline of your story—is also a part of God's story. (You knew I would get back to him eventually.)

So, what is God's story? Do you know it?

We could start with "Once Upon a Time," though "In the Beginning" seems appropriate.

In the beginning, there was God, whom we could actually call *Three Who Is One*. This *Three Who Is One* would later be called "God the Father," "God the Son," and "God the Holy Spirit." But for now, let's allow that he's a great mystery and simply call him *God*.

A Character Study

I've been using labels like "protagonist" and "antagonist," but in the very best stories, a writer turns those simple labels into multidimensional characters. Whether they're telling a story about Mother Teresa or Adolph Hitler, writers dig into the details of who the character is, his background, his influences, his motivations, how he sees himself, how others see him.

If we're going to understand the bigger story your story is a part of, we should do a quick character study about the One called "God" in that really big *first* story. What do we know about him?

If the ancient writers are to be believed, then we can put together quite a portrait about the God who created everything. Let's start with a few obvious things. He existed before everything else. He is described as creative, even before we know anything else about him. He is all-knowing and all-powerful and infinite. In some accounts, he appears to be nothing more than a tribal deity, specific to one group of people. Mostly he is seen as relational in his encounters with humanity. At times he comes off as a sovereign king, at times like a father, sometimes like a lover. Whichever way we describe him, we know he is interactive, rational, and reasoned. He is organized and ordered. He is strategic. He is both outside of time but also completely engaged in history. He is merciful even while being just. He can haggle like the best Middle Eastern merchant and come down hard like the hammer of a blacksmith.

To those who don't know him very well, he has been described as demanding, jealous, vengeful, petty, fearsome, powerful, intrusive, punitive, warlike, severe, stern, even indifferent.

For those who claim to know him well, he is all of the above *and* a source of blessing, a protector, a vindicator, a gift-giver, a provider, a champion, a healer, a savior. Above all he is Love. (Love is all those things, isn't it?)

By "Love," I don't mean that God merely loves, in the sense that he created love and it just happens to be one of his character traits. I mean, he *is* Love. Everything you know—and don't know—was created by Love. You love because he is Love. And you should put aside the romantic hearts-and-flowers Shakespearean kind of love (though that's a form of it). I mean he is the totality of the truest and purest Love that is greater than anything we can comprehend as human beings. We only ever get tiny glimpses of what such a Love looks like, feels like, thinks like, acts like. We hear echoes of it. We have brief thoughts of it. And yet we still can't grasp that God is *completely* and *totally* Love.

Dr. Sean Innerst[1]

God is Love, and out of that Love, which expresses the essence of his being, comes this creative work, which gives life to you and me and to every good gift which he supplies. That central affirmation, that central truth of faith, is the root of everything—every human possibility, the answer to every human longing, the supply for every human desire. It's all there in this central belief that God is, in himself, Love.

And it's because God is Love that he is also something else we don't usually think about: God is *limited*.

The Rules

The best stories in the world have coherent and consistent rules, even if they're sometimes revealed as the story unfolds. Whether it's *Star Wars* or *The Avengers*, *To Kill a Mockingbird* or *Moby Dick*, *Winnie-the-Pooh* or *The Lord of the Rings*, the characters inhabit a world of rules. Those rules create the questions that keep us engaged in the story. What will happen after Cinderella's magical slippers change at midnight? Will Frodo and Sam get the Ring to Mount Doom? Will Romeo

---

1   Dr. Innerst's quotes are from *The Search* video series.

and Juliet get together? Will the Avengers thwart Thanos? List the best stories you know, and you'll find that the author has established rules that make up the reality of the story's world—and those are part of what keeps you engaged.

Break those rules and the audience would feel cheated. For Cinderella to suddenly say, "I'll just wiggle my fingers over my glass slippers and say a few words like 'shooby-dooby,' and they won't change back to ragged shoes at midnight," would be frustrating. Imagine an alien spacecraft suddenly appearing at the pinnacle of Mount Doom and zapping the Ring with a destructo-ray to save Frodo and Sam. That would be silly. Stories that have tried such things usually disappear into a literary oblivion (or become a cult-favorite because they're so bad).

What's all this have to do with God? Simply this: God created rules for the story that he follows.

Heavy Lifting

A lot of people have asked the question: "Can God create a rock that is so heavy that even He can't lift it?" If the answer is yes, then they say, "Ah! But that means God isn't all-powerful." If the answer is *no*, then we have to admit that there is something God can't do, which then means he isn't all-powerful. Let's stop messing around with trick questions and get to the real issue: *Is God limited?*

The answer is a qualified *yes*. You see, God cannot contradict his own nature. He is Truth, so he cannot lie. He's not capable of it because it is not in his nature to do it, much as you can't snap your fingers and turn into an Egyptian pyramid.

In God's story, there are rules he has created and, remarkably, he respects those rules. A lot of people don't get that. Which is why, when things get really bad and our world is filled with intense suffering, someone will say, "If there is a God, why doesn't he fix it?" That would be a fair question if

God ignored a rule he instilled into humans: *the will to choose freely.* That will is such an important part of God himself that he didn't withhold it from the Spirit he breathed into the first human beings. Even the angels have that will, allowing them to serve and worship God—or not.

God doesn't usurp our will, even though he can. He may nudge us, whisper to us, call us, send fire from heaven to drive us, part the waters, and even stop the sun in the sky, but he won't override our will. To do so would be contrary to the very love by which he created us. Forced love is not God's love.

See the binding that holds all this together? It's very simply a love story. Love created space and time, and put you in it. Think about it for a minute: Your life is part of a love story, because God is Love. You see, just believing in God isn't enough to make your life a love story, or even a good story. The Greeks and Romans believed in lots of gods, and those gods were all egotistical [insert terrible euphemism here]. What a nightmare. The Judeo-Christian God is the only God in history who ever claimed to be Love itself, and to invite humanity into that Love. So, if you can accept that you're inside a love story, it's because all things are inside of the God who is Love.

The Story Continues

All right. Imagine that this *Three Who Is One God Who Is Love* created everything—the sun, the stars, the Earth, and all that is on it. It is, of course, perfection because he is perfect. And then imagine that he has placed a garden in this world to be a home to his greatest creation: the creation made uniquely in his image. (Let's not quibble over how long this took—in a snap of his fingers or over the course of billions of years. Nor over what the literary meaning of "garden" was. Just stay with me for the overarching story.)

As he fashions this greatest creation of his, he breathes into it his Spirit with his attributes: an eternal soul, a will to choose, reason by which to choose, intellect, imagination . . . and love.

This creation, which is traditionally called *man*, is meant to be an eternal companion for God—a "partaker in the Divine Life"—not because God needs anything, but because the God Who Is Love wants to share that Love and to have his creation know and share that Love in return.

Imagine that. Man is uniquely both flesh and soul, matter and spirit. Nothing else in creation—not the angels nor animals nor amphibians nor creepy-crawly things—can claim that. And as I said before, man isn't a spirit that happens to be trapped in a body, or a body that happens to contain a spirit. Man is created to be both.

God also creates *woman* to be no more or less than man. The woman and the man are complementary, with distinct but important roles to play in the bigger story. They are meant to be united in a physical and spiritual mystery—just as the *Three Who Is One God* are united in a Great Mystery. The image and likeness of Love is stamped on them in a mind-blowing way. And the beauty in that union is like a finger pointing to the *ultimate* love story.

God looks at his creation and declares it "good."

What could possibly go wrong?

CHAPTER TEN

WHAT DOES GOD WANT?

You know this story. Or maybe you don't. Let's go on . . .

As mentioned earlier, an essential element of any story includes a protagonist. Who is the protagonist in the story of the Bible—that is, in the story of human existence, your story? What if the protagonist isn't us? What if it's *God*? If so, then we have to ask: What does God want? What's his mission?

Taking the story at face value, it's a love story. The God who is Love wants to be in a loving communion with the people he created.

But as with any great love story, the beloved is free to reject the love. To run from it. Or to receive it. Or in a truly great love story, the beloved is rescued and then makes her choice. And *that* is the love story of the Bible.

Dr. Ben Akers[1]

The apex of God's creation is the creation of man and woman, made in the image and likeness of God. God created Adam and Eve, our first parents, in a perfect relationship with himself, in perfect friendship with them.

---

1   Dr. Ben Akers is an assistant professor of theology and assistant dean for student life at the Augustine Institute in Denver, Colorado. His quotes are from interviews for *The Search* video series.

Their intellects were ordered to the truth, their will was ordered to the good, and their passions obeyed the will and the intellect. Adam and Eve had a wonderful relationship of communion between each other. Eve didn't have to nag Adam to take out the trash, because Adam anticipated her needs. And they had a perfect relationship, living in perfect harmony, with creation. They had stewardship of creation. This is what's called the four harmonies, the four Shalom, the four right relationships. This is God's Plan A. God created Adam and Eve to be in the Garden of Eden to attend it, to love one another, and to love him. There is a beautiful image used in Scripture to describe this reality: that in the cool of the day, God would walk with Adam and Eve. This is what God's plan was for his creation. It's a loving plan. This was what God wanted from the beginning: perfect happiness, loving relationships.

So, in this story, the all-powerful Lover sets the stage for his beloved. And it's not a cozy cottage somewhere, or a gothic mansion. It's the *universe*. (Yeah, I know. That seems a little overdone, but then, a love this great can be extravagant. Over the top.) The Lover created us male and female to give us an up-close experience of what love is, of who he is, and of the paradise waiting for us. He created the male and female to live in perfect harmony with each other, with the world around them, and with themselves—just like the Lover is the *Three Who Is One*. Perfect harmony.

So why would the man and woman mess it up? Why would someone living in perfect harmony want to choose something else?

Like every classic story, there is conflict. The conflict is usually between the protagonist and an antagonist. Remember, the antagonist is a person or force in a story that actively works against the protagonist's efforts.

Is there an antagonist in this story? Let's take a look.

One Day in the Garden

The man and woman live in this Garden—a Garden that contains beauty and order and wonder at every turn. They have free reign of it—*except for one thing*. There's a particular tree that God calls "the tree of the knowledge of good and evil" (Gen 2:9). Interesting name.

We can ask a lot of questions about this tree and what it means that it contains "knowledge of good and evil." But for all our questions this much is clear: the tree was there, and God told the man and woman, "But of the tree of the knowledge of good and evil you shall not eat, for in the day that you eat of it you shall surely die" (Gen 2:17).

There you have it. Even in the most glorious and perfect situations, there is peril. And the reason for the peril isn't so much the existence of the tree as it is the existence of a will to choose. To eat or not to eat: that is the question! The man and woman have options. Would they yield to the reign of Love over them? Or did they want to be like gods? Or course, God had already made them like himself, and would give them *more*, but did they want to have something else on their own?

We don't know how much time passed between the instruction not to eat of that tree and what happens next. It might have been hours, days, months, years. What we do know is that the man and woman were in the Garden, it was their home, and God had given them responsibility to take care of things. But things were about to change.

Enter the antagonist.

Another Character Study: The Cunning One

In a play, we might now read the words "The Serpent enters, stage left."

Is it literally a serpent that can talk, like something out of Disney's *The Jungle Book*? Maybe. Or it might be a figurative phrase, similar to how you'd call a man a "snake" for his double-dealings. It is some kind of a created beast; we know that much. And we can presume that the beast was created good, because everything was, and that he "beast-i-fied" himself somehow. And we know that the serpent is described as the most cunning of all the creatures made by God. Being cunning, by the way, isn't the same as being smart or wise. If you ever watch a real snake seek out and capture its prey, you are seeing a good visual for the word "cunning." Yet, at the same time, snakes can also seem downright stupid.

Let's go to a character study about the serpent. There are a lot of theories about why this being is called a "serpent." In the ancient world, serpents—which comes from the Latin *serpentum*, meaning "snake" or "creeping thing" (serpents were any category of reptiles without limbs)—were considered an enemy to mankind. You can imagine, in a part of the world with a lot of desert, how a serpent would not be welcome. You can imagine the regular real-life horror stories of Bedouin children running and playing only to have their life cut short because an adder's head popped out of the sand and bit their ankle. Game over.

The ancient Egyptians believed in a gigantic snake called the *Apophias*. It threatened to capsize the boat of their sun god. But they also used a snakelike form for the author of physical and moral evil called *Typhon*. In their symbolical alphabet, the serpent represented cunning, lust, and sensual pleasure. And Norse mythology taught that a giant snake wrapped itself around the earth, what some would call a symbol of the sea itself. And then there's the Hebrew account—the one we're talking about—where the *nahash* causes problems in the Garden.

But rather than dwell on the physical form, let's go to the character it obviously points our imaginations to: Satan. The Devil. Ancient writers have called him the "adversary," the "accuser," "a liar and the father of all lies." But who is he? To figure it out, we have to piece together accounts from the ancient sources, like the Bible, along with traditions, legends and the conclusions of the best minds over two thousand years of history.

What we know is that Satan entered the drama a long time before he appeared as a serpent in the Garden. And by "a long time" we don't mean the day before, or years before, or ages before. It was before time existed. In that non-time, God had created beings called "angels." These were purely spiritual beings, not flesh and blood like us. They were created to be assistants to God, attending his throne. After the creation of our world, they became messengers of God to mankind, our protectors and the facilitators of God's work. They're actually organized like the military, with ranks and job titles and specific duties.

These angels weren't just robots. Like us, they were given free will, the ability to choose. They could serve God, or not. They could obey God, or not.

Satan was one of those angels—one of the top angels, in fact. He wasn't called "Satan" then. He was actually called "Lucifer"—which is a word meaning "brilliance" or "shining star of the morning." He was the best of the best. But he wasn't satisfied with that. He had serious ego problems. He was jealous of God, even envious. He thought he could be a better God than God and decided to take the position. And legend has it that in the dumbest miscalculation in military history, he actually gathered an army of angels together and revolted against his Creator. (Of course, any sin can be considered a similarly stupid, miscalculated rebellion.)

The coup failed. Satan lost. And as punishment, he was thrown out of heaven, which is why he is often called a "fallen angel."

And then when the created world we've come to know and love comes along, God created a Garden and the man and woman. And there's where *Satan Also Called Lucifer Appearing as a Serpent* shows up, stage left. And hating God, he set his sights on God's image and likeness: us.

The Pivotal Scene

The serpent asked the woman: "Did God actually say, 'You shall not eat from any tree in the garden'?" (Gen 3:1). What a great trick question.

The woman corrects the serpent. "We may eat of the fruit of the trees in the garden, but God said, 'You shall not eat of the fruit of the tree that is in the middle of the garden, neither shall you touch it, or you shall die," she explains (Gen 3:2–3).

It's interesting that the woman added to God's prohibition. He said not to eat of the fruit, but she added that even *touching* it would cause trouble. Was she already positioning God as being unreasonable and demanding? People looking for an excuse to reject God often do this, don't they? How many times I've heard things like, "The Church is so repressive! All they ever do is guilt people and talk about rules, rules, rules!" (For the record, I've been going to church my entire life and can count the number of "fire and brimstone" sermons I've heard on one hand. Funny.) Maybe Eve was just looking for her excuse. She couldn't find one, so she made one up.

Au contraire, the serpent said (because we happen to have a French actor playing the part). *Au contraire!* "You will not surely die. For God knows that when you eat of it your eyes will be opened, and you will be like God, knowing good and evil" (Gen 3:4–5).

And suddenly the fruit of the tree looked very enticing to the woman. She looked at it with an intensity that resembled pure lust. She *desired* it with everything in her being. So, she took some of the fruit and ate. Then she turned to the man, who was nearby, probably watching a football game and not paying attention. She shared the fruit with him, because man likes to eat when he watches football.

At that very moment, everything changed. "Then the eyes of both were opened" (Gen 3:7).

Ashamed

The phrase "the eyes of both were opened" doesn't suggest that they were blind before, but that they now saw things differently. And as soon as their eyes were opened, the man and woman were ashamed of their nakedness.

Had they not noticed before that they were naked? Maybe not, because their nakedness was completely normal and beautiful and perfect. It would not have occurred to them to cover up for modesty's sake. Sex was pure, the desire for sex was untainted. But all that changed. Their eyes were opened to their nakedness. They were so ashamed that they made some makeshift clothes out of the foliage.

But this story isn't just about modesty and floral fashion. In that very moment, when the man and woman made their choice, all of creation changed. Something that wasn't supposed to be there had now come in. It was like an infection, the kind of infection that would devastate everything God had created.

What was it?

Death.

Dr. Sean Innerst[2]

It's a horrible tragedy. They're to blame for all the sad things that have happened in human history since. God never willed that from the beginning, but he had to allow for the possibility of it because he wanted human beings who can love. So, they have to be free. And unfortunately,

---

2   Dr. Innerst's quotes are taken from interviews for *The Search* video series.

Adam and Eve freely said no to that offer of continual integrity, harmony, peace, and beauty that they had received from the open hand of God.

Welcome to the Beautiful Graveyard

Death now entered the perfect world of the man and woman. And according to the rules of this world, death isn't merely the cessation of life, since the man and woman were created as eternal beings. Separation of body and soul is painful, but the worst death that entered the world was spiritual death—a separation of the soul from God. It's the vast, horrible, painful space where God isn't. They had definitely rejected the Lover who had created them.

There's no way to overstate the significance of this plot twist. All of humanity, even nature itself, was changed by this single event. It changed the relationship between the man and the woman, between them and God, between all living things. Death came in as the ultimate contagion, the supervirus in the mainframe. It arrived as a total disruption in the DNA. Man and woman were created to be eternal—and now they are infected with the curse of death. What happens to an eternal being that is now going to die, but can't because it's eternal? Myths about vampires and zombies explore this question. Imagine being cursed to live forever, but dead at the same time.

God Knows

According to the story, the man and woman knew they'd blown it. Not only did they throw together some clothes to cover themselves up, but they did what small children often do when they've been naughty: they hid.

But where do you hide in a Garden like that? And how do you hide from the One who created all of it? They tried anyway.

Here's the official narrative. The man and woman "heard the sound of the LORD God walking in the garden in the cool of the day" (Gen 3:8). Scripture says God was "walking"—maybe strolling, enjoying the Garden's beauty, or maybe he was searching for them. And the man and the woman hid among the trees, or maybe behind the very tree itself.

God called out to them, "Where are you?" (Gen 3:9). Make no mistake. God knew where they were, but he wanted them to come out on their own, as a choice. Think of a Lover coming home to the beloved, knowing full well that the beloved had been unfaithful. *I know you're here. Come out and face me.*

So, the man stepped out and admitted that he heard God coming and was afraid because he was naked, so he hid himself.

"Who told you that you were naked?" God asked, already knowing the answer. "Have you eaten of the tree of which I commanded you not to eat?" (Gen 3:11).

The man replies in what would become an all-too-predictable way: he throws the woman under the bus. He said, "The woman whom you gave to be with me, she gave me fruit from the tree, and I ate" (Gen 3:12).

God then asked the woman: "What is this that you have done?" (Gen 3:13).

And the woman, not do be outdone by the man, also passes the blame. She said, "The serpent deceived me, and I ate" (Gen 3:13).

God then leveled his gaze at the serpent, who was still hanging around, probably to enjoy the way he'd screwed up God's creation and fatally wounded the two things God loves more than anything. You see, scholars and theologians have speculated that the serpent—Satan, the fallen angel—was motivated by pure jealousy and hatred. He was repulsed by the idea that God would dare to create a creature like man, a creature that is both flesh *and* spirit and, worse, the very center of God's love. That's why he did the one thing that could hurt God more than anything else: he lured them into disobedience. You can be sure Satan was thrilled, smiling even as he cowered (if a serpent can do either). Any punishment from God was worth enduring for what he'd succeeded in doing.

Consequences

God must follow the rules he has created. The man and woman made a choice and, as we know, choices have consequences. The consequence for the serpent was to be cursed to an existence of constant misery, wallowing in the worst sins of pride, covetousness, anger, envy and a host of others. Satan and the legion of fallen angels that had followed him would replay this scene over and over throughout history, hating mankind, wishing to devour every last one of them, while envying all the things mankind has that they don't. The result? God declared that the serpent would strike at man's heel, and man would bruise the serpent's head.

The consequence for the woman is to suffer great pain in childbearing—as if the joyous act of bringing new humans into the world would now be a reminder of the curse she's unleashed by her choice. And her relationship with the man becomes adversarial, one of both love and conflict.

The man, who went along with the woman, will suffer the consequences by having to work and sweat to eat. No more strolls in the Garden. He is now at odds with nature itself. Instead of enjoying the fruit and abundance of the Earth, he'll have to deal with thorns and thistles. His entire life will be one of hardship, until he physically dies.

The Lover banned them from the place of love, but he didn't abandon them.

The creation is ruined by the stain of sin. Everything now stinks of death. The divine life that man was meant to have with God is fractured. Satan knows God won't or can't break his own rules to fix it, so Satan wins.

What can God do?
That's what we'll call a *cliff-hanger*.

CHAPTER ELEVEN

BROKEN

You might think of that whole story as an ancient fairy tale. Or maybe you think it's literally true. Maybe it's something in-between. But here's what we can conclude for certain: mankind is broken.

When something is made for one purpose and is used for something else, it breaks. When my kids use the microwave as a fork warmer, things break. We were created by God and for God—by Love and for Love. We chose not-God. This is where the love story that is your life has taken a tragic turn. We are the fork in the microwave.

You might not believe in God, but everyone has to acknowledge this part of the love story. Mankind is broken. Separated from the Love we were born to find, we share our brokenness with everyone around us, sometimes breaking ourselves—or them—even further. Don't believe me? Look at your own life experiences. Look at your tendency to be drawn to things that are destructive, your temptations, your selfishness. Watch the news.

We want to blame God for it all. How often do you hear people say, "Hey, God! If you're really there, why are children starving in Haiti?" I think God is looking down from heaven, saying, "I was about to ask you the same question."

And no amount of education or money or sex or enlightenment has been able to fix what is wrong with our very natures. We are at war with ourselves. We are at war with each other. The very best of what we are is in constant conflict with the very worst. We are suffering from the fruit of good and evil. The will is impaired. Passions are disordered. Abundance and bounty give way to thorns and thistles. Harmony yields to disharmony. We call this the Fall of Man.

Dr. Sean Innerst[1]

People ask: "If the universe is good, if everything God creates is good, then where does evil come from? What about the tragedies of human experience? What about all those things against which we rightly rail: injustice, poverty?" All of those things were introduced by human waywardness and sin. They don't come from God. I often tell people that we don't live in the world God made. We live in the world we have made of the world God made. God created a good world—holy, perfect. He can do nothing else, because he's a perfect God, a good God, a loving God. He creates free beings who are capable of saying no to the goodness that he has provided in the world. And that's really the root of evil. When we ask the question, "Why would God create evil?" we really ought to ask the question, "Why do human beings create evil?" It's going to require the whole of the biblical story to solve that problem. And God is going to have to enter human history again to solve the problem set in motion by our original sin.

We can't fix our break with God. We can't fix the chasm between us and the Love and Life we were made for. We can't

---

fix the reality of death. Turns out we're not the protagonist-hero in this story after all. So, what can be done?

Help has to come from somewhere else.

God in the Machine
The early Greeks had a funny way of rule-changing in their plays. It was called *Deus Ex Machina*, meaning "God in the Machine." The way it worked was that a playwright would tell a story and get the characters into predicaments they simply couldn't get out of. Then, suddenly, a big box would be lowered from above the stage, and one of their many gods would step out and fix all the problems.

We have to admit, there's something about the "God breaking in to the story to fix things" narrative that answers a deep longing in our hearts. But stories are representations of life, and we all know that life rarely has easy fixes. In the real story of God and the Garden, there would be no easy out. God was going to break in to the story, but he wasn't going to break his rules, waving his all-powerful hand to make everything as it was before.

So the story is stuck right where it is. Satan had his victory over God by deceiving the man and woman, persuading them to reject God to become, in essence, their own gods. As a result, death entered the world and these beings, meant to live for eternity in a divine life with God, were now like the walking dead, but with better motor skills and articulation. (They were not alive the way they were, but not quite dead yet.) They were disconnected from their true selves, separated from their truest Love, and from the happiness they were made for.

What was God supposed to do?

Going Forward

From this point on, history shows us how the relationship between God and mankind moved in the kind of trajectory usually found with extreme roller coasters. Though the descendants of mankind rejected God and stayed at odds with him, they still had that spark burning deep inside that yearned for something beyond themselves—a deep memory of what had been lost in the Garden. Sadly, they tried to compensate for the loss of their One true God by following other gods, in the vain hope of trying to fulfill that yearning.

But God didn't let the story end there. We're in a love story, remember? Not a nightmare. Looking back through history, as chronicled in the Old Testament of the Bible, we can see the pieces God began to put into place to save us. God had a plan.

Figuring It Out

Back in the fourth and fifth centuries a man by the name of Augustine (referenced earlier as "AP") wrote his *Confessions*. It became one of the most profound and insightful autobiographies written then, or since. In it, Augustine, an African of Roman heritage, details his spiritual journey. As a typical young man, educated in the classic Roman fashion, he had an expected disdain of the Christian beliefs that had become prominent in his world. For example, he admitted to having a deep prejudice against the Bible—a book his own mother revered as being divinely inspired. But Augustine thought it was boring and, worse, a jumble of contradictions. He considered its style of writing unworthy to bother with, especially when compared to someone like Cicero, whose use of the Latin tongue was stirring.

But then Augustine met Ambrose, a man of great intelligence who was also a Christian bishop. Ambrose caused Augustine to think twice about the Bible. *How could someone as smart as Ambrose believe it?* Augustine wondered. So, he dug into the Bible for himself.

As a child of Roman thinking, Augustine had no issue believing in God. Even a great thinker like Aristotle believed God existed. But the Bible claimed to be a collection of books orchestrated by God himself, chronicling God's specific interactions with man primarily through the nation of Israel. This was a problem for Augustine. He couldn't fathom that God had actually made himself known through history, or had ever intervened in its course. That required a level of faith that, philosophically, he wasn't sure he could accept.

Augustine wrestled with the same kinds of questions we wrestle with now. If God can transcend the limitations of time and space, then why would he involve himself in petty human affairs at all? Why would he speak in the plain language of the Israelites, through nomads with little education? It was beneath God to do such things. A Creator-God would surely be too great, too sublime, too majestic for all that, wouldn't it? (He had not yet considered that Love is the most sublime and mighty Reality of all.) Augustine wrestled. And yet, Augustine couldn't dismiss his own attraction to what he was learning. Something within him *wanted* it to be true.

The Mystery

One thing Augustine came to understand was that a great "mystery" was behind God's work in history. In his famous book, *Confessions*, Augustine didn't just wonder about the mysteries of the universe; he wondered about the mysteries within his own heart. He reflected on various decisions he had made throughout his life, admitting more than once that he had become a puzzle to himself. He had a nagging hope that just maybe the God-man story in the Bible was the missing piece in his puzzle of human brokenness and existence and longing.

Now Wait Just a Minute

All this talk about the Bible is nonsense, some say. It's all superstition. The Bible's accounts of God's miraculous deeds in history are no different than the fantastic stories you'd read in the mythologies of ancient pagan religions. Just swap God out with Zeus or Poseidon or any other pagan god, and it amounts to the same thing.

Augustine thought that way too. But something changed his mind.

Another Look

Augustine had read many of the great philosophers of Roman times in his search for wisdom. He tried to read the Bible, but he was initially put off by the translation he'd been given, dismissing the whole thing as "unworthy to be compared to the majesty" of other writers.[2] Later, he would join a school of thought that took great pride in criticizing the Bible, arguing that it had been corrupted along the way. But he still sensed that he was missing something, and he wished that someone would challenge their criticisms. He was sure there was another perspective he wasn't getting.

Finally, a respected speaker took up the task and effectively refuted many of the arguments. Augustine was impressed, but not enough to explore the Bible more fully. As time went on, Augustine realized that all of the great philosophies and ideas around him still weren't giving him the answers he needed about his life and his yearning.

Fast forward to Augustine's encounter with a Catholic bishop named Ambrose, who impressed him with his overall kindness and eloquence of speech. Typically for Augustine

---

2   St. Augustine, *Confessions*, Book 3, Chapter 5, translated by F.J. Sheed (New York: Sheed & Ward, 1943), 46.

(and a lot of us), he was impressed by Ambrose's style, but not the substance.

Over time, Ambrose presented solid answers to the criticisms Augustine once held about the Bible. Augustine realized that the Bible was not something that could be "grasped by the proud" nor laid open to childish minds, but was "shrouded deep in mystery."[3] He reached a point where he knew he should embrace the Truth he was finding there, but he kept putting it off.

Now I'm at the moment in a garden that I described in chapter 1. Augustine was visiting with a friend and was overwhelmed by the emptiness of his life. He felt nagged by a desire for something else in his life, but he kept putting off what he knew he should do. Weeping, he slipped outside to the garden and collapsed under a fig tree. He was miserable. He called out to God, asking, "How long, how long shall I go on saying tomorrow and again tomorrow? Why not now?"[4]

This is one of those moments when I wish God had shouted out an answer, like a blast of thunder. But God didn't. Just the opposite. From somewhere over the garden wall, Augustine heard the voice of a child chanting the phrase, "Take up and read."[5] He thought it must have been part of a game, but he couldn't imagine what game would have such chant. Then he accepted that maybe God himself was answering him. *Take up and read.*

He rejoined his friend inside the house, picked up a Bible there, and read the words of the Apostle Paul: "Not in rioting and drunkenness, not in chambering [debauchery] and impurities, not in contention and envy, but put ye on the

---

3   Ibid.
4   St. Augustine, *Confessions,* Book 8, chapter 12, translated by F.J. Sheed (New York: Sheed & Ward, 1943), 178.
5   Ibid.

Lord Jesus Christ and make not provision for the flesh in its concupiscences [lustful desires]."[6]

The words spoke directly to Augustine's heart. Like a man proposing to his beloved, offering her his very life, Augustine knew it was time to make a decision.

The Library

Augustine soon realized that the Bible wasn't simply a book to be read in the same way as other books. To treat it as a textbook, or as a history book, or even as literature is too limiting. The Bible is actually a library of books. And as with any library, you have a wide variety of genres and styles represented. There are historical accounts, poems, parables, letters, transcriptions, allegories, and legends. Figuring out which is which is the challenge, but it's not an insurmountable one.

For example, the accounts that should be read as history are fairly straightforward, even though ancient writers did not chronicle history like writers do now. They weren't journalists. Historical accounts were sometimes condensed, chronological details were moved to fit a theme, and passages were paraphrased or summarized to capture a key idea rather than give a verbatim account (though the tradition behind any paraphrasing or summary had to remain true to what the speaker said). The New Testament is made up of four accounts of the life of Jesus, and yet we wouldn't call them biographies in the strict use of the term.

Still, the Bible is an astonishing collection. For it to have been written across the span of hundreds of years and continents, by people of diverse educational and cultural backgrounds, and remain true to a central, unifying theme is a miracle. And for many of the stories to be simple enough for a child to grasp, yet deep enough for mystics to marvel over,

---

6   Ibid, 179. The quote is from the Apostle Paul's letter to the Romans, chapter 13, verses 13-14, as translated by F.J. Sheed in this work.

is a wonder unto itself. What other book can claim such a thing? Some have argued that only God himself could make it happen, moving and inspiring the writers in a uniquely supernatural way—which is why he is considered its primary author. And that's why it's called "the Word of God."

A Unifying Theme

What theme is at the center of all the Bible's books? Love. We see love in God's relationship with mankind. That's why I keep calling it a love story—*the* love story.

Our story about the man and woman in the Garden came from the first chapters of the first book in the Bible. There we read the consequences of their decisions. We see murder and betrayal. We see mankind spreading out, and taking the sickness of sin with it. But we also see God seeking out individuals who showed the promise of that first man and woman.

There was Noah, saved by God from a deluge to wipe the slate as clean as it could be.

Then came Abraham, called by God from his home country to another land, with an agreement that would change the course of history: if Abraham followed God, then Abraham and his descendants would be blessed for all time. They'd be a light to all the nations, God said, and through them, God would rescue mankind. That family, later a nation, bore the name of one of Abraham's grandsons: *Israel,* meaning "God will prevail."

We can leap-frog through history to another man called Moses. There's a lot we could say about him, but we'll stick to the main story you probably know: God worked through Moses to rescue the entire nation of Israel from slavery. It was through Moses that God established what we call the Ten Commandments, the foundational laws that would bring life-saving parameters to that nation and become a cornerstone of law for most civilizations. Within those laws were rituals and sacrifices to temporarily address mankind's ongoing separation from God. God led Moses and the nation to a place where they could settle down, build a kingdom, and be the promised beacon of light to all the nations around them.

Was it perfect? No. What happened in the Garden of Eden played itself out over and over again. God would reach out to mankind, and mankind would respond, often by rejecting God. Consequences followed. But God would work through those consequences to rescue mankind, only to have mankind reject him again. Two steps forward, three steps back, in a painful kind of *Groundhog Day*. And yet, in the midst of it, God was putting in motion his greater plan.

But we have to be careful, in case we fall into the same trap that Augustine experienced. We can read a clunky translation or criticize a detail here or a confusing passage there. We could find ourselves reading with spiritual cataracts on our eyes, missing the forest for the trees. We miss the profundity of love that is infused throughout every word in every book. Can I put it simply? The Bible is a book of stories about God running and scrambling to grab hold of us and bring us back to our created purpose: being loved by him and loving him in return.

God is the Lover who, against all good sense, searches the alleyways and brothels for the beloved who has given herself away. And we are the beloved, trapped in a such a place, vaguely remembering what it once was to be truly loved, yearning to escape, but not knowing how.

Augustine understood. He realized that, no matter what humans did, no matter how far off the track we went, we still had a desire within us for a particular kind of happiness, that yearning for fulfillment, for meaning, for the Love and joy eternal we were made for. If we wanted God, it was because he wanted us first and created us to want him. Even when mankind seemed to forget God completely, God never forgot mankind. Augustine was stunned to find all he had been longing for in something he'd spent much of his life dismissing as foolish.

Meanwhile . . .

What is Satan doing all this time? He's been like the warden of a prison. He's got mankind right where he wants them. Oh, there were occasional jailbreaks and rescue attempts, but nothing to worry about. Humans' fallen nature always seems to sabotage God's best efforts. And no matter how well humans behave, they are still enslaved to death.

Satan's in a sweet position. He knows God won't break the rules to save those unworthy creatures. There's no lasting hope for these creatures that God loves so much. We are severely impaired, incapable of attaining what God originally intended. He believes his victory will hold forever.

And then there's God, who knows that humans' original disobedience has to be reversed. The divine life that was shared in the Garden has to be restored. Satan's malicious jealousy has to be neutralized. Death itself has to be reversed. And to do all that, God does something that very few people, even Satan, expect.

The God of eternity enters into the confines of time and place. The God who created everything became one of his own creations. *God became man.*

Talk about a game-changer.

CHAPTER TWELVE

MAKING AN ENTRANCE

If you were a god and you had to come to earth as a man to give it a major overhaul, what would you do? Would you come with thunder and lightning, like the gods of old? Maybe show up dressed in the best clothes, driving the snazziest car, surrounding yourself with an entourage of bodyguards? Maybe you'd be more presidential and show up in a slick suit with diplomatic flags flying all over your palatial residence. How would you make your entrance?

It's easy to guess that you wouldn't want to show up as a vulnerable embryo—a baby growing inside of a peasant girl—two thousand years ago in an insignificant town on the outskirts of the Roman Empire. You wouldn't want to be a poor child born to poor parents, living a quiet life, unnoticed, normal, playing with friends and learning a trade as a carpenter, going through the rigors of manual labor, sweating out the days and having a meager meal in the evening. You wouldn't do that. What kind of God would do that?

Yet, he did. The God we've been talking about came miraculously to a young virgin who had never been intimate with a man. "Let it be to me according to your word," she had said to God's messenger (Lk 1:38). Her baby was born in a stable, virtually homeless. The devil didn't notice. He never expected God's next move to happen in a storage place for cattle. It makes no sense for God to do all that. Unless God is Love, and Love is more beautiful and otherworldly than what the devil, or we, could ever make sense of.

God came fully human to fix what the first human had broken. He would go through all of the pains and joys of humanity; this God would spare himself nothing. He came as the great deliverer—the *Messiah*. He came as the long-awaited salvation for all mankind—but not the kind anyone expected. He entered deep, deep behind enemy lines, not redeeming political nations, but redeeming all that it means to be human. He came as the one called Jesus Christ.

Jesus

No reputable historian disputes that Jesus really existed. We have mountains of textual and archaeological evidence from the first three centuries of Christian history: Jesus and the early Christians are mentioned by the Jewish historian Josephus and by pagan writers like Tacitus and Pliny. And, of course, we have the documents written by those who were closest to him: Matthew, Mark, Luke, and John. From them, we get the inside scoop about this man we know as Jesus.

Time itself is measured from the birth of this man. Countless cities are named after his followers. His image hangs in every museum and has inspired artistic movements. Some of the most iconic music ever written has been composed in his honor. In fact, there are more statues of him all around the world than of any conquering king that's ever marched with an army behind him. He has more than two billion people following him on earth now. Jesus Christ is easily the most dominant figure in all of history.

Going back to the historical record, you'll see a man called Jesus, a human with all of the aches, pains, and pleasures that come from flesh and blood, living in a fixed time (the first century) and a fixed place (the country known as Israel). His biography is simple: Jesus was the son of a Jewish woman and the stepson of a carpenter. He followed in that trade for most of his life. He lived in a village called Nazareth and, like much of the known-world, suffered under the oppressive rule of the Roman Empire.

Around the age of thirty, Jesus stepped out from his life as a craftsman to become a teacher—a "rabbi," as he would have been called.

In his first-recorded encounter with humanity in the Gospel of John, he saw two men following him, and he asked the same question we asked at the beginning of this book: "What are you looking for?" He knew that he, himself, was the answer to that question.

He assembled a group of unlikely men—fishermen, tax collectors, outcasts—to follow him as students, who were called "disciples."

It should be noted that these disciples weren't merely tagalongs who followed Jesus because they had nothing better to do. They had actually given up their livelihoods, even prosperity, to learn from him.

In ancient times, a disciple was tasked to, in essence, *become* the rabbi. They were with him constantly, to study his ways, to know how he thought, to understand the fullness of everything he said and did. They committed their rabbi's words to memory.

Remember Well

It may be hard for us to appreciate that kind of ancient learning. We think of learning as something we do institutionally—at schools, in seminars—not in the context of a 24/7 relationship with a teacher. And we wouldn't assume to memorize everything the teacher had to say. But these ancient disciples did—in part, because it was their job.

Think back. There were no printing presses or video cameras on smartphones or any other means to capture what a person said and did. Pens of a kind existed, yes—parchments and scrolls, yes—but nothing like we know now. Besides, writing was for the upper classes. So, all they had was "oral tradition." They learned by hearing and seeing and by meticulously memorizing what they'd heard and seen. And while that made learning far more challenging, it also gave education an element of depth that's hard to comprehend in today's world of quick memorization and easy Google-it.

When a disciple of the philosopher Antisthenes lost his notes, his teacher chided him: "You should have inscribed them on your mind instead of on paper."[1] It was not uncommon for students of Homer to recite all of his works from memory. Statesman and dramatist Seneca boasted that he could hear a poem once and recite it back verbatim.[2] At the end of a long day at an auction, the Roman orator Hortensius was known to be able to list every buyer, purchaser, and bid he witnessed.[3] Sound crazy? Ray Bradbury made use of the same discipline in *Fahrenheit 451*, to counter the cultural book-burning that went on in his dystopian world. Memorization as a reliable transmission of information was vital to the ancient world—especially when memorized accounts and sayings were put into writing.

That's why we have four accounts of the sayings and works of Jesus. Four men—Matthew, Mark, Luke and John—wrote what they had personally witnessed, or had learned firsthand from those who had been closest to Jesus. For them, memory was an instant-replay, as if it had happened just yesterday.

Check out what Luke, a physician by trade, said about his account:

> Inasmuch as many have undertaken to compile a narrative of the things that have been accomplished among us, just as those who from the beginning were

---

1   Jocelyn Penny Small, *Wax Tablets of the Mind: Cognitive Studies of Memory and Literacy in Classical Antiquity* (New York: Routledge, 1997), 115.
2   Ibid. Small, Wax Tablets of the Mind, 115.
3   See Pliny the Elder, *Natural History in Thirty-Seven Books*, Book 7, chapter 24.

eyewitnesses and ministers of the word have delivered them to us, it seemed good to me also, having followed all things closely for some time past, to write an orderly account for you... that you may have certainty concerning the things you have been taught. (Lk 1:1–4)

Matthew and John were both eyewitnesses of Jesus's ministry (see Jn 19:35; 21:24). Mark chronicled his account of Jesus based on the experiences of Peter, the leader of the disciples.

Whispers

Most of us have played the game "Telephone" in school. It's the one where someone whispers a statement to a classmate, who whispers the same thing to the next classmate, and so on and so forth, until the last classmate repeats out loud what the first classmate said. Often, it's hilariously wrong.

We're tempted to think that this is how it has always been in history, statements and facts getting distorted by repetition over time. We might believe, for example, that the writers of the Bible did not remember things accurately. Or maybe they were driven by a particular agenda to propagate myths and legends about Jesus.

There are several problems with those theories. One is that the commonality of the four accounts, which were written in different times and places, is evidence of a common memory of experiences. Second, the writers were living in a time of great persecution. To proclaim themselves as disciples and, worse, to write publicly about Jesus's deeds and words meant arrest, suffering, and even death. In fact, the earliest Christians had nothing to gain by testifying to Jesus's life, and everything to lose. Three of the four writers were martyred for following Jesus. Why would they do that?

Dr. Brant Pitre[4]

We have more historical evidence about Jesus of Nazareth than we have about most other ancient historical figures that people never call into question. The historical legitimacy of Caesar Augustus, Pontius Pilot, and King Herod the Great isn't doubted. In fact, if you look very carefully at the New Testament itself, the four Gospels of Matthew, Mark, Luke, and John are actually four ancient biographies written in the first century AD, within the living memory of Jesus himself, by people who were either eyewitnesses to Jesus or the companions of apostles, such as Mark and Luke. And there's no other historical figure with four biographies written within his lifetime that any serious historian would call into question, let alone argue their existence or compare them to myths of Santa Claus or the tooth fairy. Even atheist scholars, some of the most skeptical scholars in our day, have argued that the evidence for Jesus's existence is not debatable. It's simply not a question that serious scholars have asked.

Remarkable Credibility

In general, historians accept the credibility of the accounts, even if they disagree about some of the more remarkable events within them. Thomas Jefferson created his own version of the New Testament, cutting out the miracles because they didn't fit with his "Enlightenment" view. But make no mistake: Jesus did remarkable, miraculous things.

When Jesus traveled and taught throughout Israel, he didn't simply preach. We know from the four accounts that he validated his words with "signs." He healed the sick from all kinds of illnesses, he miraculously fed thousands of people, and he told waves on the sea to be quiet and they calmed down.

---

4   Dr. Brant Pitre is Distinguished Research Professor of Scripture at The Augustine Institute in Denver. His quotes are taken from interviews for *The Search* video series.

Most remarkable of all, he told dead people to get up and they came back to life. Jesus did all these things, not only out of love and compassion, but also to prove that his words were true.

Not everyone believed. For some, nothing Jesus did was enough. The same is true today. As we've already said, belief, like disbelief, is a choice.

Who Do People Say That I Am?

The Gospel accounts report an interesting, and important, conversation between Jesus and his disciples. The context is that the disciples had been out teaching and preaching, and when they returned, they had a kind of debrief with Jesus. Then came a question. "Who do people say that I am?" Jesus asked (Mk 8:27).

It was an intriguing question. Jesus had been teaching and performing miracles that touched people to the very core. Now he wanted to hear the "word on the street." Who did everyone think Jesus was?

The disciples gave their answers. "John the Baptist," said some (Mk 8:28). John the Baptist was a man who had preceded Jesus by calling people to repent of their sins, and demonstrating it by being immersed (baptized) in water. He had been beheaded for speaking out against a Jewish ruler (making us wonder if the people thought John had escaped death, or was actually resurrected). The other disciples chimed in. Some of the people believed he was one of the Old Testament prophets—Elijah, maybe Jeremiah, resurrected. Clearly, the people saw Jesus as more than just a teacher or philosopher.

Jesus then put the question to the disciples themselves: "But who do you say that I am?" (Mk 8:29). There is an important implication in this question. If the public perception of Jesus was accurate, it would have been easy for Jesus to say, "Well done! That's who I am," and then go on from there. But he didn't. He wanted to know what those closest to him believed.

"Who do you say that I am?"

That question echoes down the centuries to us now.

You Are . . .

True to his character, the disciple named Peter dared to answer the question directly. Peter was always doing things like that—stepping up first, sometimes putting his foot in his mouth. And this question was huge. It was like a pass/fail pop quiz.

Peter answered differently than the others. Peter, who'd been with Jesus day in and day out, witnessing all he'd said and done, now offered the most breathtaking option possible. He proclaimed: "You are the Christ, the Son of the living God" (Mt 16:16).

The Christ

Within the culture of Israel—the very Israel that gave us the story about mankind's break from God—the people understood that God would send them a person specially chosen to reestablish their relationship with God spiritually, and the kingdom of Israel physically. He would come from the line of the most valiant King David and make all things right again. In this person, the promises that God had made over the centuries would be fulfilled. This man would be the "anointed one"—known in Hebrew as the "Messiah," and in Greek as the "Christ."

That's what Peter proclaimed. Jesus was the Messiah—and not only the Messiah, but the "Son of the living God." For the people at the time, to be a son was to be equal with a father. Peter called Jesus the deliverer, the savior, who was *equal* with God himself.

Had Peter lost his mind?

To call Jesus a worthy leader or a prophet was one thing, but to call him *God* was something else, something terrible. It was blasphemy. According to the law, blasphemy was worthy of death.

Worthy of Death

The fact is, Peter was reiterating what Jesus had said time and time again in his teaching. He was no ordinary man, he told the crowds. He even dared to apply to himself the sacred and unspeakable name that God had used when talking to Moses hundreds of years before.[5] It was no mistake or misunderstanding. The religious leaders knew what he was saying and wanted to kill him for blasphemy.

As if that wasn't enough, Jesus said again and again that God was his Father in heaven. They understood what he meant well enough. To be the son of a dog is to be a dog, by nature. He was telling them (and us) that he is *God the Son.* The religious leaders wanted him dead. Not because he challenged the status quo. Not because he was a political revolutionary. But because he was "making himself equal with God" (Jn 5:18).

I'm sure some of Jesus's followers wanted him to backpedal and say, "Wait a minute. I'm speaking symbolically, metaphorically, allegorically. I mean 'Son of God' in the way that we're all 'children of God' because we're part of humanity and he loves us like a father." But he didn't. He upped the ante, doing things that only God could do, like forgiving a paralytic man's sins. Those nearby rightfully reacted. "Who can forgive sins but God alone?" they cried (Mk 2:7). Jesus didn't argue. He simply pushed his point further by saying, "But that you may know that the Son of Man has authority on earth to forgive sins . . . " (Mk 2:10). And then he turned to the paralytic man and

---

5   See the third chapter of Exodus, the second book in the Bible, when Moses asked God to identify himself. God proclaimed, "I AM WHO I AM" (verse 14), and reiterated to Moses, "Say this to the people of Israel, 'I AM has sent me to you.'" In Jn. 8:58, Jesus answered a challenge from the religious leaders by announcing, "Before Abraham was, I am."

said, "Rise up, pick up your bed and go home" (Mk 2:11). And the lame man did.[6]

Jesus put the religious leaders into a fearful rage. They went from zero to hatred in no time at all.

A Terrible Misunderstanding

It's been fashionable over the years to say that Jesus was misunderstood. Really, he was just a good teacher, a moral philosopher. The people got a bit confused, that's all.

Authors G. K. Chesterton and C. S. Lewis both knocked that idea on its head. They argued, essentially, that Jesus could not be a good teacher and still claim all of the other things he claimed. What "good teacher" would dare ask his followers to put their lives on the line for him? What "good teacher" would state, as Jesus did repeatedly, that he was worthy of worship? Jesus even dared to proclaim that he, himself, was the way to heaven in the afterlife. "Trust me with your souls," he said.

What kind of "good teacher" would do that?

Jesus was *not* a good teacher, both Chesterton and Lewis argued. If Jesus claimed things that he knew weren't true then, at best, he was a gifted and eloquent *liar*.

Lewis went a step further and added that if Jesus wasn't a liar and actually believed he was the Son of God, then he had to be a lunatic.

And if Jesus was either a liar or a lunatic, then those who gave up their lives to follow him were deceived by him, or deluded themselves.

Let's think about that. Many of Jesus's followers maintained their faith in him all the way to gruesome and torturous deaths.

That's quite a misunderstanding.

But we're missing the third option. He was a liar or a lunatic . . . or he was who he said he was: *God in the flesh.*

---

6   See Mt. 9:1–8; Mk. 2:1–12.

Blessed Are You

Let's go back to Peter and his answer to the "Who am I?" question from Jesus. "You are the Messiah, the Son of the living God" was Peter proclaiming that God himself was right there in human form. The eternal and immortal God was fully present in this man they had come to know and love.

How did Jesus respond? Did he correct Peter and say, "No, no, you got my metaphors and analogies and my symbolism all wrong!" No. He said, "Blessed are you. . . . For flesh and blood has not revealed this to you, but my Father in heaven" (Mt 16:17). In other words, Peter didn't come up with this idea on his own. It was revealed to him by God. And there we see the amazing relationship between faith and truth. The spirit placed within Peter because of his faith in Jesus now connected to the One who gave him that spirit and revealed a life-changing truth.

Who Do You Say He Is?

This is where we have to pause and ask the question, "Who do *you* say that Jesus is?"

If you want to hold to the implausibility that Jesus was simply a good man or a good teacher, a radical or a misunderstood philosopher, a visionary or merely a first-century spiritual leader, then it's just as well that you stop here. You can put Jesus on that list with any number of people who have lived and died for what they believed. But if you do that, then the rest of the story won't make much sense. In fact, there is no "rest of the story" about Jesus, or about your life—you're stuck where you began, with the same nagging questions and insufficient answers.

Or you could ask, "What if he really was the divine Son of God who walked among us in human form? What if he is the One through whom the whole world was created, and who entered his creation to fix what was broken? What if he is the answer to that yearning for happiness and fulfillment and meaning? What if heaven is real as he said it was? And what if he is the answer to the question 'What are you looking for?'"

I mean, if God is Love and Love came to save you, then there's no reason to look elsewhere. Why would you, if he's the answer to what you're looking for? If God is Love and Love came to save you, then even when life is at its worst, there is a deeper meaning and purpose to it all. The pains we experience now are not much compared to the eternity the God of Love has set up for you. The end of the story corrects all of the twists and turns you face now. The pages of everyday life, even when they're frayed and tattered and worn, are bound into the chapters of the greater story of eternal Love. If Jesus is who he said he was, then the story we're really looking for when we yearn for love and a happy-ever-after dream is *true*. It's yours. Take it.

If that worldview isn't the foundation for a truly happy, purpose-filled life, I don't know what is. It sure beats the "I'm a cosmic accident destined for nothingness" worldview.

Dare you hope it's true? Will you allow the possibility that Jesus is who he said he was—Love's answer to our hope? If so, then there's more to the story. And it's not pretty.

Remember the rules? God the Lover has to undo what was done by the first man and woman in the Garden. It's not enough to wander around Israel healing people and offering wise sayings. He has to give up *everything* to rescue his beloved.

Dr. Sean Innerst[7]

St. Augustine says that the whole biblical story from beginning to end is for the purpose of revealing God's love. And he focuses the expression of that love in Jesus Christ,

---

7   Dr. Innerst's quotes are taken from interviews for *The Search* video series.

who comes at the very center, not only of the biblical story, but of the whole of human history, dividing it effectively into two parts, BC and AD. He came to bring meaning and purpose to human life, to save us from sin, but also to provide us with a revelation of the truths about who God is and about who we are. The whole of the biblical story is brush strokes revealing the portrait of Jesus Christ. And that painting happens throughout the Old Testament, in Adam, in Noah, in Abraham, in Moses, and in David. They are living prophecies of Jesus Christ himself, prefiguring him. And when Jesus comes, he discloses the full meaning of those Old Testament figures and everything God was doing with them in that record.

Christ is the central purpose and meaning of everything. And this painting is being revealed in your life, too, if you have the eyes to see him. We find the full revelation of the divine Love: that God isn't satisfied with creating us and leaving us to ourselves, but enters into human history and the nitty-gritty of human life, actually becoming one of us in what we call the Incarnation. Through him we have new life. And that's the great gift, the great story, the great narrative that the Bible tells of a God who doesn't stand off at a distance, but who enters into the very grit of human life, into its fabric, taking it to himself and, finally, lifting us into the heavenly realm.

CHAPTER THIRTEEN
THE ULTIMATE SACRIFICE

Let's summarize our story so far. God created mankind to have an intimate and eternal relationship with him. Mankind was (and is) persuaded by Satan that it's better to go their own way, to *be* God—thus, betraying the relationship with God and introducing death to mankind.

God couldn't break his own rules to fix the situation, so he had to do the unexpected: become man to reverse the curse of disobedience and, ultimately, death.

In the first century, in a little Middle Eastern country called Israel, he did just that in the person of Jesus Christ.

Now we have to tell the hardest part of the story.

A Battle to the Death
Shortly after the story when Jesus asked the disciples, "Who do people say that I am?" and Peter proclaimed that Jesus was "the Messiah, the Son of the living God," Jesus had to deliver some terrible news: He would be handed over to the people who wanted to kill him. They would succeed in their mission. Jesus would suffer and die.

But there was good news, Jesus said. After three days, he would rise from the dead. Love would win.

Imagine how shocking that had to be for the disciples. They've just confirmed that Jesus was the "Son of the living God"—only to have Jesus tell them he would suffer and die. Talk about a head-turner. And Peter, being Peter, started to argue. It won't happen. It *can't* happen. We won't let it happen! Poor Peter.

Jesus countered with a stinging rebuke: "Get behind me, Satan! For you are not setting your mind on the things of God, but on the things of man." (Mk 8:33).

Why did Jesus call Peter "Satan"? Well, one theory is that Jesus was resisting yet another temptation from the original and greatest of the tempters. Remember the serpent in the Garden? Well, he appeared to Jesus during a forty-day outing in the desert and tried to tempt Jesus away from his mission. So, the ancient liar would certainly use the good intentions of someone like Peter to try to thwart God's plan to rescue mankind. Jesus smacked down the suggestion. He was determined to do what he'd come to do.

I can sympathize with Peter. The Messiah was supposed to come in great victory, overthrow the oppressors, and set things right again. But no, God had to achieve victory over death itself. To do that, he had to conquer it from within—changing its very meaning by taking it up into himself. It must have sounded to Peter like a great mistake. To die meant being executed on one of Rome's most horrific forms of punishment: the cross.

The Cross
After nearly two thousand years, the cross has become the most well-known symbol of the Christian faith throughout the world. It represents salvation and new life. If you give it some thought, though, it's crazy. It's like celebrating the image of a hangman's noose, an electric chair, or the syringe for a lethal injection.

In the time of Jesus, the cross was the ultimate symbol of humiliation, subjugation, and death. Those sentenced to be executed that way were more likely to commit suicide given the choice.

The cross was not only a means of execution but a way for the Romans to incite terror among its citizens. "Whenever we crucify the guilty," one ancient Roman writer wrote, "the most crowded roads are chosen, where most people can see and be moved by this fear."[1] The threat of crucifixion helped to keep the world under the Roman Empire's iron rule.

That's what Jesus, the *Perfect God Become Perfect Man*, had to do: die on a cross. So, just in case you hoped God's fix was going to be a wrist-slap or some token symbol of punishment, it wasn't. It was brutal—the worst kind of death. Let me explain it to you.

First, the ordeal began with a scourging. Various historical accounts describe this as being so severe that rib cages, spines, muscles, and entrails could be seen through the flayed skin. The condemned would then carry a crossbeam weighing upwards of one hundred pounds on his back, 650 yards *uphill* to the place of execution. Stripped of his clothes, he would be jerked backward to the ground, where the crossbeam would be attached to the main part of the cross. Square-cut iron nails were hammered through the soft parts between the hands and wrists to the crossbeam. Then the right foot was placed over the left foot and pushed slightly upward so the knees were slightly bent, another nail hammering them both to the wood behind. The cross was placed upright, with the condemned pushing up on his nailed feet to alleviate the pain in his wrists, or dropping down to alleviate the pain in his feet, all the while being stretched out to intensify the inability to breathe properly, his head moving back and forth, up and down, under a blistering sun—Romans called this "the dance of death." This continued for hours and hours as insects attacked the condemned's wounds, fatigue invaded his entire body, his muscles cramped, and every part

---

1   Possibly Quintilian in Declamations, 274; quoted in Martin Hengel's *Crucifixion* (Philadelphia: Fortress Press, 1977).

of his body screamed in agony.[2] That is what Jesus—and the disciples—knew would happen.

Another Garden

If we filmed our story, we would now use the script term "cut to" and jump to a scene of Jesus in another garden called the Garden of Gethsemane. It is night. Jesus, who has just had a final meal with his disciples, is now praying in the garden alone. He knows what is going to happen next: one of the disciples will betray him, soldiers will come and arrest him, he'll be dragged to the religious leaders who will accuse him, and the Roman governor will concede to his execution.

In storytelling terms, this is the beginning of the "climax." The climax, as you may remember from school, is when a character reaches a point of no return and the conflict reaches its highest point of tension. Everything that happens in the rest of the story depends upon this moment.

Jesus is at the point of no return in this garden. He is praying, agonizing over the torture that he is about to endure. His very humanity screams at him: *Don't do it! There must be another way.* He prays that the "cup" may pass from him (Mk 14:36).

The "cup," Jesus well knew, was the "cup of wrath." Unlike other cups in biblical imagery—the "cup of righteousness" or the life-giving cup Jesus had offered to his disciples in their last meal together—the "cup of wrath" would be the full consequences of mankind's sin against God, the horror of excruciating death.

We might think of that first garden, where the first man made a choice. Now, Jesus is making a choice. The first man, and all to follow, chose to disobey God and gave up life for death. Jesus, God the Son, must now choose to obey God and endure death to bring us back to life.

Will he or won't he do it?

---

2   See Jim Bishop, *The Day Christ Died* (New York: Harper & Brothers, 1957).

Jesus prays with such intensity that he sweats blood. "Remove this cup from me," he begs (Lk 22:42). But he knows there is no other way to rescue mankind. He must freely sacrifice himself to fix what was broken. And he must go deep into the pit of misery to redeem the darkness we all have to walk through in life and death. A light will shine in the darkness for us when all other lights go out, but only if he'll go there. He *must* go there for us.

He prays to God the Father: "Not my will, but yours be done" (Lk 22:42). He echoes the words his mother had said to an angel thirty-three years before: "Let it be to me according to your word" (Lk 1:38).

The choice is made. The fully fury of death would be unleashed upon him.

Why?

Can we fully grasp the idea that God came to earth to die for an unworthy race of humans?

The religious leaders of Israel certainly couldn't. Years after Jesus died on the Cross, the Apostle Paul—a man who had actively tried to eliminate the Christians—acknowledged that the cross was a scandal, complete foolishness to the pagans, a stumbling block to the Jews. The notion of a crucified God was preposterous.

Yet, the cross ultimately reveals the deepest truth we've been exploring about God. Its horror is Love's answer to our hope. Love caused God to create mankind, love caused God to do whatever it took to bring mankind back to him, and Love put Jesus on the cross. It turns out that God is *Love* after all.

On the dark hill of Golgotha—locally called the "Place of a Skull" (Mt 27:33)—the blinding light of God is truly revealed. He's the One who continually scrambled after us through our ages of rebellion. Those who were paying attention could look at him and say, "So, it was you the whole time."

And it's on that terrible hill that God reveals who *we* are: small specs in a corner of the Milky Way Galaxy—dirty, confused, messy, broken little people. But for all that, God reveals that we're worth *dying* for. Pause a moment to think about it. What is your net worth? *God*, apparently.

Crowds passed him by as he hung there. *All* of human history passes by the cross at one time or another. As you gaze up on him, you can hear him ask, "Who do you say that I am?" The answer determines who we say we are, what we're worth, and what the story of life is ultimately all about.

A Reminder

Let's look back to our earlier character study of God. He is Love—not as a characteristic or an attribute, but as Love itself. When Jesus offered himself on the cross, he did it from the same Love that was present when God first created the universe—and mankind.

The Apostle Paul explains it this way:

> Christ Jesus, who, though he was in the form of God, did not count equality with God a thing to be grasped, but emptied himself, by taking the form of a servant, being born in the likeness of men. And being found in human form, he humbled himself by becoming obedient to the point of death, even death on a cross. Therefore God has highly exalted him and bestowed on him the name that is above every name, so that at the name of Jesus every knee should bow, in heaven and on earth and under the earth, and every tongue confess that Jesus Christ is Lord, to the glory of God the Father. (Phil 2:5–11)

For the Apostle Paul, this was the summation of what had happened. In another letter, he wrote:

While we were yet helpless, at the right time Christ died for the ungodly. Why, one will hardly die for a righteous man—though perhaps for a good man one will dare even to die. But God shows his love for us in that while we were yet sinners Christ died for us. (Rom 5:6–8)

But the story doesn't end there. The tale of Jesus's life and death is wrapped up by a three-word sentence that changed everything. And by everything, I mean, *everything*. It was news so good I don't think it was initially shouted, but whispered. The first people to carry the news could barely believe the words coming out of their mouths.

Could it really be true? The tomb was empty. "He has risen" (Mk 16:6).

Love wins.

Dr. Ben Akers[3]

God reveals his great love for us in sending his Son to us. Every act of Jesus as he walks the earth is an act of Love. When he heals the lame, when he gives sight to the blind, when the deaf hear, when the dead are raised from the dead, these are acts of Love.

Then, God shows his greatest Love for us on the cross.

The cross shows us what that Love looks like in history. The Son becomes man, and he does what he's been doing for

---

3   Dr. Ben Akers is Associate Professor of Theology and Associate Dean with the Augustine Institute in Denver. His quotes are from interviews for *The Search* video series.

all eternity, he gives himself to the Father in Love, holding nothing back out of Love for him and out of Love for us.

What the cross teaches us is what we need to learn. We are called to enter into a communion with the God who is Love, we will be saved by Love, and we are saved by the Son, who pours himself out in Love on the cross so that we can become like him. We must pour ourselves out in Love, by his grace on the cross. Only then can the relationship that Adam and Eve had with God be restored. Jesus did that for us. It's a gift of Love, from God to us.

CHAPTER FOURTEEN

PUTTING THE PIECES TOGETHER

Do you see how it all ties back to where our story began? God created us in his image, according to his likeness (Gen 1:26). We were made to share in his divine life—and the Love that is himself. But sin disrupted God's design, infecting us all. Jesus came as the "New Adam" to conquer that disobedience through obedience (see Rom 5:15; 1 Cor 15:45).

Jesus shows us what it means to be "fully human"—to be the image of God—by pouring out his life in Love. Jesus shows us that the greatest tragedy can be transformed into a means of salvation. His death becomes a gift of Love.

More Than Death
The twist in the story is that Love had to hit death head-on to undo what had happened back in the Garden. But dying wasn't enough. A lot of people have died. There's nothing special about dying, even if you die for a noble cause. Jesus had to do more than simply die.

The four accounts in the Bible tell us explicitly that Jesus suffered a terrible death on the cross. The disciple called John, and the author of the fourth Gospel account, was there to witness it. We can hardly grasp the horror of it. And when Jesus breathed his last breath, no one looking upon that lacerated body doubted the finality of his death. It was God's answer to the question "How much do you love the people you made?" Look at the cross. *That* much.

And then, three days after his death, a group of women went to the tomb where he'd been buried—and it was empty. Peter and John looked for themselves. He was gone. The disciples gathered. They conferred. And then Jesus appeared to them himself—in the flesh. He ate with them. They touched his wounds. He hadn't come back as a ghost—he was flesh and blood, risen from the dead. It was confounding. The One they had seen nailed to the cross, the One who had a spear thrust into his side to make sure he was dead, was alive again.

That's how it had to be done. It wasn't enough to die. Death itself had to be conquered. The only way to do that was for Jesus to die brutally on the cross, with no doubt that he was dead, and then fully and physically rise from the dead again. Only then could the curse of death in the Garden be undone.

And Satan, who thought he had everything locked up tight, was outmaneuvered. His victory became the worst possible defeat. You, me—all of humanity—were given a second chance, a new life.

No Words

How do we get our minds around the finality of death being undone?

Think of the person you love more than anyone in the world, lying on a cold slab in a mortuary. You could gaze upon the body, heartbroken, knowing without a doubt that the life that had once filled it is now gone forever. Moments of love, laughter, tenderness, and intimacy will never be experienced again. Not in this life. It's over. There's a funeral, maybe a last glance at the body in the coffin, a graveyard, and the deep, cold hole in the ground as the final "resting place." You've had to say your goodbyes and, with an ever-growing emptiness inside, you step away. In the days to follow, you expect your loved one to walk around the corner or come down the stairs, and you ache because it won't happen.

Think, now, of what you would feel if, three days later, your loved one is suddenly standing in front of you, not only alive, but living with a radiance of health you've never seen before. You might be startled, doubtful, frightened. You've seen the movies. Is this a zombie? A vampire? Something horrible? But it becomes clear that it isn't. This is not a terrible trick; it is your true love, risen from the dead and returned to you, fully alive—even *more* alive.

How would you feel?

This is the reality of Christ's resurrection. And it is reality for those who live in Christ. Death may separate us, but not forever. Death no longer gets the final word. Neither does sin. Or pain. Or crying. Or suffering. Or broken humanity. Ultimately, God "will wipe every tear from their eyes" (Rev 21:4). Christians can accept death as a part of our condition, but not because we've made peace with it. Certainly not because we surrender ourselves to the void—like the depersonalizing religions of the East who consider such a thing "enlightenment." We do it because we can look death in the eye and say, "Jesus won. Your days are numbered."

The Love Story

Have I mentioned that God's story is a love story? (You know I have. And I'll keep saying it.) God is not some entity, with a lot of rules and doctrines that seem to have nothing to do with your life. Hold on to the love story. It's not only the biggest and greatest love story, but a love story that includes you. It's a love story that wraps every page of your life in his life, death, and resurrection. It's a story that shows us not only who he is, but who *you* are.

When you see your life as part of that love story—a love you don't deserve and could never earn—then you're seeing the Love you were made for, the Love that changes everything. Every part of *your* story is redeemed by God's love. An illness, a divorce, abuse, failure, betrayal, even your own sins—if you are in Christ, those all become just pages in the bigger story. Many of the pages might look the same, but there's a different cover on the book: *Love Story!* This view of life is what has made Christians throughout history unconquerable. They had a joy that didn't depend on people, a peace that didn't depend on circumstances, and a hope that not even death could take away. They were living in a bigger story.

The bigger story shows that you were created by a God who loves you, who found you worth dying for, who has forgiven the worst possible thing you've ever done, who has destined you for eternal glory.

This is the true *meaning* we've been talking about. Only when you embrace it can you have the happiness, the joy, the fulfillment that you've looked for and that mankind has been looking for since we first gazed up at the night sky and wondered what it all meant.

And the best part of this whole story is that it's all true—every single word of it.

Yeah, But . . .

You might be skeptical. That's understandable. Let's answer some final and really important questions about Jesus. Note that I didn't say, "Let's remove all your doubts," because facts only lead you to the threshold of faith. Then it's up to you if you want it, or if you want to stay outside.

For centuries, skeptics have tried to explain away the story of the resurrection. Like the religious leaders who masterminded the crucifixion, the skeptics claim that it's a lie, a story of make-believe; Jesus died, but the body was stolen by the disciples so they could claim he had risen from the dead.

Some have claimed that Jesus did not actually die on the cross but was only unconscious and, after lying in the tomb for some time, suddenly woke up—like the "mostly dead" Wesley from *The Princess Bride*. The skeptics argue that the disciples saw this "awakened" Jesus and got confused. They didn't understand what had happened and foolishly insisted he had risen from the dead. And for some reason, Jesus didn't correct them by saying, "No, really. I was only knocked out for three days. It's amazing I didn't bleed to death in that damp and dark cave. And, boy, did I have a hard time moving that big stone that had locked me in the tomb, but, hey, it's not like a crucifixion takes away a person's strength."

Others claim the resurrection story developed out of a case of mistaken identity. The disciples saw someone who looked like Jesus and incorrectly thought he'd risen from the dead. But it's hard to imagine how the disciples, who'd spent three years living with and following Jesus, mistook a stranger as their beloved rabbi and hope. It's worthy of a Monty Python movie.

None of the theories hold up when you look at them closely. No credible historian accepts that Jesus survived the crucifixion—especially when you consider the brutal beating he had to endure *before* he was nailed to the cross. They recognize the absurdity to believe that the Roman soldiers, professional executioners who would have been severely punished for bungling the job, somehow failed to kill Jesus.

But let's consider the popular claim: that the resurrection was a hoax invented by the disciples. Maybe they did it to prop themselves up, or to keep from looking stupid after their leader had been executed, or maybe they were simply deranged. The problem is that the disciples weren't just a group of people who could believe what they wanted and freely go around preaching it to others. It wasn't the age of "hey, it's okay what you want to believe." Just the opposite: to do so meant imprisonment, suffering, and even death.

To teach that Jesus had risen from the dead, knowing it was a lie, would be insane, since the religious leaders had them targeted for persecution. (And most people would have spotted that kind of madness in the rest of their behavior.) We know from history that the Romans eventually punished and killed professing Christians as insurrectionists. So, why lie about such an unbelievable story—and then die for it? What's the incentive? People who lie generally have something to gain.

Let's go a step further. *If* the disciples were to invent a story about the resurrection of Jesus, it certainly wouldn't look like the one we find in their accounts. For one thing, the first witnesses to the resurrection were women. Women, in those days, were not regarded as reliable witnesses. It's ridiculous to start there.

For another thing, the disciples didn't initially believe Jesus had risen from the dead. Why add that to your story? Or, for that matter, why mention the part where Peter, the lead disciple, *denied* that he even knew Jesus? If you're going to make up a story like that, you'd want to get rid of those kinds of details. It's bad PR otherwise.

The more one studies the accounts and the data, the less it looks like a made-up story. In fact, the best historical explanation for the empty tomb—the one with the fewest problems—is that Jesus did what he said he would do: he rose from the dead.

If he didn't, then we're exactly where we were in the beginning. Or, as the Apostle Paul wrote to one of the early churches: "If Christ has not been raised, then our preaching is in vain and your faith is in vain. . . . If Christ has not been raised, your faith is futile and you are still in your sins" (1 Cor 15:14, 17).

That doesn't mean we have to believe what happened purely as a matter of faith. Jesus's resurrection, which conquered death and verified all he said about himself, was seen by *eyewitnesses*.

Case Closed

Harvard Law professor Dr. Simon Greenleaf was determined to debunk Christianity.. He said that everything these crazy people believed rests on their claim that Jesus rose from the dead. He said their testimonies would never hold up in court. So, he started studying the accounts as ammunition to make people aware of how ridiculous Christianity was.

He never made it. He became a Christian.[1]

Oops.

What happened?

It was the rules of evidence used in any court case that won him over. He knew that credible witnesses to a crime would always lead to a conviction. Especially if there are a *lot* of witnesses. There were. Case closed.

What if the witnesses were threatened to be killed if they upheld their testimony? Then, surely, they'd think twice about lying and would certainly recant. But they didn't recant, and so they were killed.

Greenleaf concluded that the Christians didn't give their lives for a philosophical system—all kinds of people have done that throughout history. The Christians died to uphold what they *knew* because they had *seen it with their own eyes*. Think about it. Had it been a lie, then why die for it? Yet, one after another, these eyewitnesses gave up their lives defending the truth they had *seen*: Jesus Christ crucified and risen from the dead.

Thirty years after the crucifixion of Jesus, Peter was tried in Rome and sentenced to death for his faith—death on a cross. So, reasonably, if the resurrection of Jesus was a lie and Peter, of all people, knew it, then that would have been the time to admit it. But he didn't. Instead, he asked to be crucified upside down, since he wasn't worthy to be crucified like his Lord. What

---

1   See Simon Greenleaf, *An Examination of the Testimony of the Four Evangelists: By the Rules of Evidence Administered in Courts of Justice, with an Account of the Trial of Jesus* (London: A. Maxwell & Son, 1847).

a horrible way to die. But I have to note: the place where he breathed his last, upside down on that cross, is now St. Peter's Square in the Vatican.

A Global Phenomenon

Jesus appeared in Israel to be the Jewish people's long-awaited Messiah. That being the case, and considering his death, you'd expect the whole story to have stayed localized, with a cult growing there and remaining among those people. But the story of Jesus skipped the borders and spread throughout the non-Jewish world.

We could credit the effective missionary work of those first disciples, using the network of Roman roads to travel far and wide with their message. That's too easy. Historically speaking, the idea that other nations would worship the puny God of the puny nation of Israel was outrageous. At the time, nations closely identified with their own gods. To worship the deity of another people would be, in effect, to declare that other nation superior to one's own. It is no wonder, for example, that the Greeks insisted that the Jews worship their god Zeus when they conquered Jerusalem (see 2 Macc 6:2).

Likewise, the Greek pantheon had a quick makeover after the Romans rose to power. Zeus became Jupiter, Poseidon became Neptune, and so on. The Romans made other gods their own. So, to imagine the nations of the world worshipping the God of a relatively irrelevant country like Israel was unrealistic.

Consider, too, that Israel was a minor player in the scheme of things. The surrounding nations all had much greater civilizations. In many ways, their cultures were far more developed and impressive. Their armies were far more powerful. In sum, if you were to bet on all the world worshipping the gods of one of any of these nations, it certainly would not have been Israel's.

But it happened. Two thousand years after Jesus, here you are, living on the other side of the world from where historic Israel existed, hearing about an event that never should have gone beyond the boundaries of that time and place.

Dr. Brant Pitre[2]

Were ancient people more gullible and credulous than we are today? Did they believe things that we know better than to believe?

If you look at the actual historical evidence, and the historical scope in the writings of the Jewish nation, then you'd see what can only be called a fulfillment of prophecy. If you were a Jew in the first century AD, you would know that, for centuries over the centuries, prophet after prophet had claimed that one day the age of salvation would come. And when the Messiah came, they said, the Gentiles, the pagan nations, the world, would turn and convert. They would worship the God of Israel, the God of the Jews, the God of Abraham.

And you know what? After Jesus of Nazareth was crucified, died, and then rose from the dead, one by one the pagan cities and towns and peoples, starting with the Roman centurion standing at the foot of the cross, began to convert. They put away their idols, they gave up their temples, and they began to worship the God of Abraham. They're still converting today.

How do you explain that? How do you explain the fact that, hundreds of years before Jesus was born, the prophets

---

2   Dr. Pitre's quotes are taken from interviews for *The Search* video series.

had it right? Is that a coincidence? Or is it Providence? Is it a sign that Christianity isn't a man-made religion, but a God-made religion, a divinely revealed religion?

The fact is, Jesus of Nazareth is the only leader of any world religion who was ever preannounced. There are no prophecies about Muhammad, or Buddha. But there are prophecies of the Jewish Messiah, fulfilled by Jesus of Nazareth down to the tiniest detail.

In the End

The *denouement* of a literary story is what happens after the major conflicts are resolved. The word is French, meaning to "untie"—which is funny, since we usually "tie up loose ends" at this point in the story. It's the resolution of the most important dramatic questions.

But it's not resolved, is it? The bigger story is playing itself out in human history. And what about *your* story?

We began with the yearnings and desires of your heart. We've learned that they can be satisfied, in spite of the struggles you have, the obstacles you face, the suffering you endure. Your life is part of a bigger Life, created by God and fulfilled by the death and resurrection of Jesus Christ.

Pope John Paul II said:

It is Jesus you seek when you dream of happiness; he is waiting for you when nothing else you find satisfies you; he is the beauty to which you are so attracted; it is he who provokes you with that thirst for fullness that will not let you settle for compromise; it is he who urges you to shed the masks of a false life; it is he who reads in your hearts your most genuine choices, the choices that others try to stifle. It is Jesus who stirs in you the desire to do something great with your lives, the will to follow an ideal, the refusal to allow yourselves to be grounded down by mediocrity, the courage to commit yourselves humbly and patiently to improving yourselves and society, making the world more human and more fraternal."[3]

At the crossroads of time, at the center of human history, at the center of every longing you and every person who has ever lived has had for happiness, and at the center every question about how to deal with life, there is Jesus. His arms are stretched out wide, taking in every person from every time and place. He's waiting for you to respond to his invitation to join in a life beyond the limited life you have—and to start living the life you were made for.

Dr. Sean Innerst[4]

The deepest part of the human problem of sin is that it doesn't have a human solution. We're not capable of solving our own problem. As we see in the biblical story, God from the very beginning reaches down across the divide between himself and his perfect holiness and our fallen-asleep sin to provide a solution to the human problem. That's what we see in Jesus Christ. In his passion, death, and resurrection, the whole answer to the human problem of waywardness and sin has provided a grace, a power, which lifts up fallen human nature and returns us to the likeness to God that was lost through sin.

---

3   Pope John Paul II, World Youth Day Prayer Vigil, August 19, 2000.
4   Dr. Innerst's quotes are from interviews with him for *The Search* video series.

What are you going to do about Jesus?

You can look at him and walk away. You might shake your head and say he's crazy. You might catch a glimpse of him on the cross and, after shaking off the disturbing image, decide to get on with your day. I'm sure many a busy person did so on that day in AD 33. They had other priorities, after all. And he didn't fit.

Or you could admit that he's the One you've always been looking for.

What he doesn't allow is for you to walk away indifferently, without giving an answer. Yes or no—the choice is yours. What will you say to him? Who do you say that he is?

Point of Decision

I believe that once you decide for Love, everything changes. I'm not the same as the day before my wedding. Nothing in my life is. It was taken up into something bigger than me. And while countless and complex things have followed the exchange of hearts that happened on that day, it all really comes down to being faithful to the love we promised when we exchanged rings.

There are countless and complex things that come along with being a Christian too. Those things often threaten the newcomer. But as is the case with marriage, it's helpful to remember that it really comes down to the one thing: being faithful to the exchange of hearts that is the soul of any love story. Once you lose sight of that, marriage doesn't make sense anymore, and neither does Christianity.

Want to enter into that love story for yourself, now? You've just read a lot about God. Prayer is how you talk to him. You can, by a simple prayer, begin to enter the love story that is bigger than you. What are you waiting for?

Sit somewhere alone. Spend a solid minute or two imagining Jesus on the cross, looking at you with great love. Don't rush out of that moment. He did that for you, after all.

Then pray this prayer:

Lord Jesus,
You are the Love that I was born to find.
You are here, offering me your heart,
and asking for mine in return.

You have given me the freedom to say no.
I use my freedom to say yes.
I surrender all I am to you.

I renounce Satan.
Sin.
The spirit of despair.
And the lie that I am unlovable.

I forgive others, and I forgive myself
of my worst sins.
And I ask you to forgive me and to forgive those who have
*   hurt me.*

You are Lord of the universe.
Be Lord of my life.
I say yes to you.
Amen.

Want to know how to live out this love? Want to explore the life you were made for? Let us accompany you. Check out all the amazing things on FORMED.org and on RealLifeCatholic.com. Thank you for letting us take this journey with you.